GREASEPAINT & .45s

GREASEPAINT & .45s

EDITED BY RYAN SAYLES

Down & Out Books
3959 Van Dyke Road, Suite 265
Lutz, FL 33558
DownAndOutBooks.com

Cover design by Chuck Regan

ISBN: 1-948235-85-4
ISBN-13: 978-1-948235-85-3

*To Jonathon Ashley and Tom Callahan,
thank you for wanting to be a part of
this collection as much as we wanted you.
Godspeed, gentlemen.*

*Josh Stallings gave birth to this idea and even
titled it for us. Without him, if this happened
at all, it would certainly be in a lesser form.
Thank you, Mr. Stallings.*

CONTENTS

CONTENTS

A WORD FROM YOUR EDITOR
Ryan Sayles

Clowns. They mean something to everyone, whether a beloved icon of the circus or the very stuff of nightmares. They cover both ends of the spectrum, don't they? They're goofy, they squirt water out of flowers, they tie balloons, and sometimes they have fangs and eat children. I've met a lot of people over the course of my life and every single one of them has an opinion on clowns. They're like ham and pineapple pizza, or the series finale of *Lost*. There is no middle ground for clowns.

While I was stationed in Maine, there was a grown man who was so afraid of clowns that he'd literally freeze up when he saw even a picture of a clown. He'd only move his lips enough to chant, "I'm not looking, I'm not looking, I'm not looking…" When stationed in Georgia, there was a different grown man who would panic and vomit at the sight of clowns. Yes. He would *vomit*. While I was reading Stephen King's immortal book *It,* my wife would make me keep it safely stored in the freezer because she saw them do it on *Friends* and that was the only way she'd allow the book in the house.

But, on the flipside, a girl I dated in high school had a little brother who attended clown school at the local community college. It was his biggest dream. Korn wrote a pretty good song called "Clown." Back in 2010, a then-unknown director named

Jon Watts uploaded a fake trailer to YouTube about a horror movie centered around a clown *and* he had the stones to claim Eli Roth (of the *Hostel* movie fame) was producing it. Roth, who was in fact not producing the fake movie, was so intrigued by the trailer that he did indeed sign on and helped make the film. Watts has since gone on to do the latest Spider-Man movies. All because he lied about a clown. Yes, I've reduced his schooling, perseverance, training, experience, risk-taking, talent, networking abilities and much more down to a clown, but still. It was all about the clown.

Clowns go back to the ancient Greeks. It traces back to the "rustic buffoon" character type they had in their theater. That stayed in one form or another all the way up to the English harlequinade in the 1700s. A century later, a British man named Joseph Grimaldi played a character named Clown in a pantomime production that became so popular he eventually became a central cast member. Hell, for a time the character type became known as a Joey.

But then the circus came along, and they needed lovable, rustic buffoon-types to trot around and entertain large groups between other performances. So, those entertainers continued Grimaldi's tradition of whiteface makeup while they lovably stumbled through ordinary everyday tasks, fumbling them so badly that they became extraordinary and hilarious.

And then the Joker from Batman. And then Pennywise the Clown from *It*. And then *Killer Klowns from Outer Space*. And then coulrophobia, the fear of clowns. And then my wife, and then scary clown novels in the freezer next to the waffles and ice cream. And then the 2016 BoucherCon in New Orleans, which brings us to now.

Down & Out Books founder Eric Campbell was sitting at a table with several writers; that night they birthed the idea of a clown-themed anthology. Josh Stallings (Yay! Author extraordinaire Josh Stallings! Go check him out) came up with the title *Greasepaint & .45s*. Eventually I came on as the editor. The stories began to trickle in, from David James Keaton's gloriously awesome tale to Scotch Rutherford's dddaaaarrrkkk story. In between those two we got Richard Thomas's just-creepy-enough-to-leave-you-bothered vignette, Grant Jerkins' sad exploration of grief, Chuck Regan's masterful journey and R. Daniel Lester's sharp-toothed romp. And we got more, folks. We got a lot more.

In a terrible, terrible turn of events, during the process we lost two authors. In September, 2017, Jonathon Ashley, a very talented writer with five novels and numerous short stories under his belt, passed away. In August, 2018, Tom Callahan, a career journalist and college professor, passed away. Both men were very enthusiastic about the project and, while I know this isn't a fitting tribute at all, I wish I could have gotten to know each better. I would have relished working with them.

So, buckle up because there's a lot here. Clown cars, rodeos, adultery, robbery, mayhem, balloon animals, self-immolation, big red noses, cremation chambers, a funeral, kids' TV shows, lots of laughter and maybe a John Wayne Gacy reference. No, it's not my average Saturday night. It's *Greasepaint & .45s*.

Showtime.

RUBBING PETER TO PAY PAUL
David James Keaton

> *"To robbe Petyr & geve it Poule,*
> *it were non almesse but gret synne."*
> —Jacob's Well: An English Treatise
> on the Cleansing of Man's Conscience

"Clowns are not scary."

"No, they're scary, dude. I've been scared of clowns all my life, and…"

"What do you mean when you say 'clowns,' because these days assholes keep saying they're afraid of clowns, but they're always clowns that look like monsters. To this I say, 'No shit, you're afraid of an evil bozo beast with a shark mouth? Sounds like a real phobia, buddy.'"

"You don't understand, I'm talking about a normal, every-day clown that…"

"Yes, you're right, clowns with six rows of teeth that kill people and creep around the woods are scary. I agree. You blew the lid off it. Nice work, man. Your unique fear makes you very special."

"So scary, for real, dude. And it's totally a phobia."

"Hey, what's the name of that phobia where you can't stand to be around idiots who keep saying they're afraid of clowns?"

"I hate clowns."

"I hate people who say they hate clowns."

"Just keep rubbing the headstone, dummy…"

I never really hated clowns. They just confused me at first. I never understood how dozens of them could pile into that tiny VW Beetle, then drive off the stage. But then Paul explained there was a trap door in the floor, and they simply parked the car over top of it. He told me they weren't really climbing into anything, just climbing through it. So when the circus came back to town, I snuck under the tent one night and climbed onto that dark stage, and I jumped up and down, hopping two feet forward every time until I'd covered every inch of that sticky floor.

But it was solid.

When I told Paul this the next day, he said that was impossible. Then years later, he insisted I must have remembered it wrong. But I'm convinced it was the other way around.

"Do you think a grave rubbing is really worth anything?"

"Oh, definitely. I've seen people pay five-thousand bucks for a framed rubbing of James Dean's headstone."

"No shit? I tried to get a grave rubbing of Jimmy Dean's grave once myself. Felt kind of bad though, standing over that grave, wind in the beard, pondering existence and realizing it was really him down there, you know? I realized I'd never been over a tombstone I didn't deface."

"Grave rubbings aren't defacing anything."

"Okay, more like taking the face with me."

"But did you get it?"

"No, that's what I'm telling you. During my bungled attempts to transfer that legendary name onto my wrinkled sheets of parchment, I got red slashes all over the line between '1931' and '1955.'"

"Red slashes?"

"Yeah, at first I tried to rub with charcoal like you're supposed to, keep everything all neat and respectful, but it was raining so hard that it was washing all the rubs away, and I switched to crayons instead. And, man, I dare a grown man not to start giggling with crayons in his hands all serious, cemetery or not."

"Anybody buy it?"

"Hell, no. I did it in crayons, fer crissakes! Aren't you listening?"

"What did his grave look like?"

"Oh you don't believe me? Well, I don't remember too much about it, except it was covered with pennies and half-buried in the mud, like it was sinking? Three years later, I made the five-hour drive back to Indiana to try some more rubbings, but it was raining again. Tried to sell them outside the Shell station on 51 anyway, but that particular get-rich-quick scheme ended up costing me about ninety bucks in gas alone, not including the goddamn Crayolas."

"Crazy talk."

"I'm telling you, I've seen someone sell one for five thousand bucks."

"Impossible. Are you sure they weren't buying his skull?"

Even if you'll never convince me that clowns are scary, after actually being one for almost a decade, I can at least tell you with one hundred percent certainty that they aren't funny. Though Fireball Paul would have probably said different.

I'd known Paul since we were kids, back when we went to all those sweet parties together, working so hard to keep everyone entertained. That was back when we were "circling airports" together, a phrase I'll explain later. I even shared a car with him, all the way back when Fireball Paul's name was still Poindexter. Well, that was his last name anyway. His first name, like most first names around young males, meant nothing to us. And since his had too many syllables to boot, we just called him "Dexter" for about a day, then quickly switched that to "Pee" by the time the weekend rolled around, as in "The Princess and the Pee," a reference to the stain he'd left on our buddy Jay's mattress at a sleep-over when we were grade school. This sleep-over also went down in history as our very first official "Sweet Party," anointed by Paul himself. And both those names stuck to us like glue. Meaning, we just called him anything that started with a "P," and any time I attempted to plan something fun and it quickly turned to shit, it was known as a "Sweet Party," and they were typically my fault. So like if I said there was a gathering at so-and-so's house, and me and Paul got there and there was only about two people swaying back and forth in a driveway looking at their feet and no beer to be found…it was a "Sweet party, dude, thanks a lot." "Ess Pee" for short.

Tired of ruining parties, we took the party mobile instead, putting our money together to buy a big boat of a car rusting on his uncle's lawn. It looked a lot like the beast in the Evil Dead movies, only bigger, and Paul's uncle had it first.

"Do you know how many people we could squeeze in there?" Paul whispered, eyes practically pinwheeling.

It was a '71 Oldsmobile Delta 88, about as confusing a name for a car you could get, compounded by the fact that Paul's uncle called it his Banana Mobile. But we christened it The Rhino Wagon instead, because of the broken horn of a hood ornament, and that first day we must have driven around at least seven hours. Then even more the following weeks, like it was our job. In fact, we logged so many miles in that monster our hometown actually had to invent a law to stop us. The cops claimed there had always been this "cruising law" in our town, but we argued they simply couldn't stand to watch us drive around with nowhere to go. We said no law could justify their uncontrollable urge pull us over and ask what the hell we thought we were doing. And the officer at the courthouse after our first run-in with the fuzz calmly explained this law was necessary because of the people who would drive up and down and around the runways at any airstrip, waiting for loved ones to finally land but not have to pay for parking. They said the official name for the infraction was "circling the airport," and whether we knew it or not, that's exactly what we were doing. But once we heard this, we decided to adopt this phrase to describe any endless teenage fornication where we struggled to get off, then we drove around for a day to celebrate our growing vocabulary. And this name stuck, too. Neither of us could sneak away with a girl without the other one interrupting with a rap on the Rhino Wagon's window with a shout of, "Quit circling the airport, asshole! That's a hundred dollar fine plus court costs."

But we knew the cops didn't really give a shit about all our driving. They were just jealous of all the people we crammed in the back, or we crammed in the front, or crammed in the trunk, sometimes even surfing on the hood. It seemed like hundreds of limbs on the best nights, and probably sounded like even more when we cranked our horrible power ballads. Our car may have been rusty, but our speakers sure weren't.

We shared the Rhino Wagon for three years and thousands of miles, until the summer of the bubble in his brain changed everything.

"Don't dig. Rub."

"I'm tired of rubbing."

"Do it anyway."

"Why?"

"You know why. Hey, you know how much money we're gonna get? Rubbing the grave of Squeaky Pete?"

"You mean Fireball Paul."

"Whatever."

"Holy shit, look what I found."

"That's half a pinecone."

"Could be a skull. 'Yorick! I knew ye well!'"

"Why don't ya go get more charcoal from the car if you're going to fuck around."

"Did you know Yorick was a clown, too?"

"Nah, he was a jester."

"That's a clown, dumbass."

"So what."

"Did you know Hamlet was a slacker? They can tell by how old the skull of his jester was. No joke. Some scholar did the math. When the gravedigger holds up Yorick's skull and talks about him cracking jokes to make the baby Hamlet giggle, they just divided that birthday by the age Yorick died, multiplied by the Year of the Monkey or something, carry the two…and guess how old that makes him."

"How old?"

"Thirty years old, dude! That's like sixty back then."

"What's your point?"

"The point is, he still lived at home! It makes the play a whole different animal, man. Everybody always thinks Hamlet is this punk goth kid who's skulking around the castle, but he's a grown-ass man just fucking around, a midlife-crisis case, acting nuts to get out of doing any real work. Like I said, a slacker."

"Sounds familiar."

The day of the bubble in his brain, Paul was at track practice, showing off, making people laugh. Later they told me no one knew it was a stroke, and figured he was just playing dead in the middle of the high-jump pit. He was laying there for at least an hour, and then his teammates thought he was pouting about not being able to clear nine feet, so they still didn't bother checking on him for half the day. When the coach came by to clean up and found him more unresponsive than usual, he finally called an ambulance. The paramedics cut him out of his track suit and took him away, leaving the whole gutted bundle of his uniform lying in the track's inside lane, complete with a new jagged slit winding a crooked path across the chest. This is where his girlfriend retrieved it that night, a seemingly innocent gesture that ended up causing quite a bit on controversy at our school later on.

See, before the stroke, Paul was dating this moody chick named Michelle, but we all called her "Nimbus." As in "Cumulonimbus." As in "Thunderheads." As in "the dark, depressing clouds you see right before it rains." This was because she moped around like she had thunderstorm over her dome at all times. She wasn't even one of those all-black-wearing darklings you might expect something like this from either. She was small, blonde, partial to Easter-egg colored clothes, but she just seemed friggin' miserable. She drove me nuts, too, and I wasn't even dating her anymore. But Paul seemed to like her enough for both of us, and didn't seem to mind this perpetual frown painted on her face, at least for a while.

But right before his stroke, when we were driving around in the Rhino, he confided to me that he wanted to break up with her and was dreading having to actually do the deed. He told me he dreamed of dumping her almost once a day lately. And he may have pulled the trigger, if he hadn't bonked the high-jump bar at nine feet and ended up in the high jump pit with a partial loss of memory, muscular control, and the ability to speak.

When she came by my house to tell me about Paul having his stroke, I was standing in my garage and staring at her feet under the door slit and didn't answer her knocks. I'd heard the bad news already from my parents, and didn't want to have to react to it twice, certainly not to Nimbus. Instead, I waited until she drove away, and then I went through the workout routine with our weights, a routine Paul and I had carefully designed to make us the most dangerous sophomores of all time. Or at least allowed us to systematically claim enough third-place finishes in the often-ignored hurdles, high jump, and pole vault to accumulate the points necessary to get our Varsity letter jackets two years earlier than the best bona fide athletes at our school. In other words, we totally Moneyball-ed that shit, and the vice-principal actually sighed in disgust when they called our names at the letterman ceremony. We just wanted the jackets. School spirit need not apply.

When I went to the hospital that night, I saw Nimbus weeping in the waiting room, then I sat next to his bed and watched him roll his eyes trying to talk, until she ran in and pushed me aside to clutch his hand. She said she'd never leave him and that's when I realized how serious the situation actually was.

Right then, I decided it would be my mission to decipher whatever series of twitches, blinks, or grunts Paul managed to squeeze out in order to prove to Nimbus that he wanted to dump her ass. But it took weeks for him to identify common household objects on index cards for a therapists. I saw him moving his thumb for "yes." Pinkie flick for "no," barely perceptible nod for "No, that's not a hammer." I tried to explain to the nurse that maybe he couldn't identify her hammer because it was a shit drawing of a hammer, and he was probably trying to say "mailbox," but they just kicked me out.

And during all this, I had to suffer through Nimbus and her baby talk, giving him crayons, feeding him Jell-O. It all made me furious, like she was doing it to me. Sulking near his right arm, I explained it was no easier to write with a crayon than it was to write with a pen. But over on his left arm, she proved me wrong by peeling a blue one and rubbing it over the bed sheet covering Paul's hand. But when the image slowly took shape under the blue streaks of her crayon, it revealed Paul's hand giving her the middle finger. I'd taught him that one.

She ran out crying, and in came the parents. Paul's parents, my parents, her parents, everyone's parents were looking at me like I was a villain. Except for Paul. He surprised everyone by reaching for my hand. That's all I needed. I swear, if angels existed, I would have heard them singing.

The next visit I got there early, and they let me stay in the hospital room alone with him, so I asked the million-dollar question.

"Hey, do you want me to tell her to fuck off?"

By this time, he was saying a couple words and moving his left arm and left leg a bit. But for his answer, he just shook his hand "no" like it was on fire. I wasn't sure I translated this correctly, so I repeated myself.

"Just give me a sign, man. Anything."

He kept with the head shakes, so I said: "Remember all those hours driving around with her, never able to pull the trigger? Now's your chance," I leaned in and whispered. "I will dump her for you, I swear."

His next response was a little more complicated because, unknown to the nurses and physical therapist, we'd already come up with a variety of hand twitches for communication. Actual sign language was out of the question, of course, because that stuff was hard to learn, but I'd done some homework, grabbing some documentary on Marcel Marceau and watching him do his "Bip the Clown" mime bullshit, and the Ouija board I brought in was crucial, so when he wiggled his thumb up, down, up, right, down, left, up, I was surprised to translate…

"I said, 'no.'"

Okay, there was a chance he was trying to say more than that, or something else entirely, like, "Why is there a scuba diver on that wall?" (which there wasn't), but this last "No" was all I needed, so I vowed to leave her alone, let her soak up the attention for a tragedy. I promised to stay out of it. And when we had more time alone days later, he twitched his thumb around the Ouija board to spell out something else: "Sweet party, bro. This your idea?"

* * *

"Did you hear about all the clowns jumping out of trees and trying to scare people?"

"Are they dressed as clown clowns or, you know, colorful monsters?"

"We've been through all this."

"Apparently not."

"It's the same thing."

"God damn you."

"Did you see that movie about that killer clown is getting remade? Now that's a scary-looking clown. But there was something about the original killer clown guy that's gonna be hard to top."

"If you say they have some 'big shoes to fill' I might bury you here."

"It's true though."

"And for the record, no, it's not the same thing."

"What's not the same thing?"

"Don't you understand? If they were real clowns hiding in everybody's trees, no one would give a shit."

"What the fuck is a real clown?"

"Hey, was that thunder?"

"Yes, I think it's going to rain."

"Well, rub faster."

"Don't worry. One thing doesn't always follow the other."

Back at school, all that month, I started noticing Nimbus shuffling through the hallways, carrying what seemed to be a bundle of bloody rags wrapped around her schoolbooks. Behind her in the lunch line, I got a closer look and saw it was Paul's track suit, and she'd been cradling it all day. She'd carefully sewn it back together where the paramedics had cut it off his body, her bright red threads stitching up the ragged trail that had divided the front so everyone knew she'd repaired it. But these thick, red threads clashed with our blue-and-white school colors, and she sewed all these weird extra circles into the front, an unnecessary flourish that turned his track uniform into what could only be described as a costume, like something you'd find in the circus. I followed her to her lunch table, confident with every step I'd regret what I was about to do.

"Whatcha got there, Nimbus?"

"Don't call me that."

"What's this?"

"All four food groups."

"No, I mean right there. The pile of shit under your math book."

"A superhero uniform!" she said proudly. I was so annoyed I didn't even groan and said the word "groan" instead, and her friends started to chew on their lips, angrier by the second.

"But what's up with the stitches?"

"What are you talking about?"

"I'm talking about this clown suit…" I said, trying to grab it, and then her friends were around me, one of them hissing down my neck.

"What the hell is wrong with you?"

"What the hell is wrong with her?"

One of the girls shoved me, but I ignored her, not understanding why other weren't horrified by her conspicuous display. But every table within earshot was glaring at me in horror, and I panicked. I grabbed a handful of tater-tots from off their nearby trays, and I began to juggle. And the damndest thing happened. All the glares began to slide off their faces, frowns turning upside-down, as they say.

I was a natural.

"Did you ever notice it always rains when she walks by?" I said, and people were laughing. I should have stopped there.

"Oh, by the way, Paul was going to break up with her before this all happened!"

Then they were booing, and the tater-tots slipped through my fingers one by one, and the science teacher with the face like a tomato was leading me away by the arm. But not before I snatched the track suit right off her tray.

I asked him sincerely, "Haven't you ever noticed a change in the weather when she's around?"

He just yanked harder. The science teacher always liked me, up until that day anyway. And you'd think a science teacher would have noticed an atmospheric phenomenon like that.

The next day my locker was trashed. Graffiti calling me every name in the book. And when I say "in the book," I mean in my schoolbooks, too. Bunch of rotten fruit cups in my Varsity jacket pockets. Streaks of what I hoped were dried saliva on everything else. It was bad enough for the school to finally start assigning padlocks and combinations after that. So kinda like the law against "Circling the Airport," that's another legacy we left behind. Lockers finally getting locks.

I took Paul his track suit in the hospital, after I may have tried it on, once or twice, and even though it was a struggle, he climbed out of his bed to try it back on. He'd lost so much weight he was swimming in it, and he knew it. But we were walking now, and we danced down the hall best we could, and he made all the kids laugh. He was good at that.

"Did you hear about that gorilla they shot at the zoo?"

"Oh, yeah, everyone was talking about it."

"Lots of conversations lately about that gorilla. I heard they killed it to protect some dumb kid who wandered into the cage. Did you hear that? Well, luckily, I've solved this problem for everyone."

"How so?"

"Gorilla rodeo clowns, bro."

"Huh?"

"Think about it! If zookeepers want to screw around with dangerous, stressed-out animals in zoos, you just get ya some rodeo clowns."

"You might be making sense for once."

"Seriously, zoos are a real problem these days. Filthy, cruel to animals. Almost as frowned upon as the circus. So bring in the clowns, man. Part of your new job description as a zookeeper should include wearing goofy-ass clown outfits and running in there with a barrel and some fuckin' balloon animals at a moment's notice. This seems like a good compromise to me."

"I'm not gonna do that, but thanks.

"Just remember it was my idea."

"How much longer is this going to take?"

"Don't worry, this show's almost over."

After eight months of intense rehabilitation at a green, happy compound somewhere tucked away in the hills of Southern Michigan, Paul regained all his motor skills and memories, with the exception of his right arm. He was never again able to raise it higher than his shoulder, but I was surprised by his recovery and—as much as I hated to admit it—maybe a little disappointed because I'd spent so much time trying to enable him to communicate with just one hand, and just to me. His mouth was a little slacker than I remembered, too. And he seemed to spit a lot, like something in this throat didn't work quite as well anymore. Or maybe he just lost that part of the brain that reminded him to swallow. Or it could have been a new allergy? The doctor said that new allergies and aversions cropped up sometimes after strokes, so maybe he just got a little allergic to me, because whenever I asked him about his feelings for Michelle, I mean "Nimbus," back before the bubble in his brain, he'd just spit and change the subject.

They were together for another year, and I shouldn't minimize how effective she was in helping him recover. She brought in all these old 45s, and we listened to them through all his exercises. I'd hated her taste in music when we were together, but now it didn't bother me so much. Anything that helped Paul, helped us all. Hey, that shit rhymes.

When they both started college in Cincinnati the following spring, I didn't see either of them that much anymore for quite a while. But, ironically, they broke up anyway, without my help at all, right about when his right arm started twitching again. And he came back home to us, wearing that track suit, and still swimming in it.

But the best thing that happened after that summer of the bubble in the brain was we didn't have to go into the Army anymore, even though he'd signed all the necessary paperwork weeks before he blew that fuse in the high jump pit, even though I'd called to meet with a recruiter myself, the day after he told me this. We had mixed feelings about not serving our country, but I reassured him that at least we broke up with Uncle Sam easier than we broke up with Nimbus.

"Dodged a bullet, you could say."

He laughed, but I never really talked to him about how I was still ducking the Army recruiter's phone calls ever since his stroke. No way I was gonna do it alone, right? That didn't make any sense to me. It was like that band we almost started back in the sixth grade, with all our joke songs like a poor-man's Weird Al. We quickly realized, even doing those parodies for our classmates, that a two-man band is about as welcome as a one-man band, which is as much of a pariah as the class clown. Meaning no one really wanted to hear those jokes. We just thought they did.

The next summer, we joined the circus instead of the Army, and we were satisfied, because that shit was pretty much the same thing.

"For real, when are we gonna get to work?"

"Work? Hey, if I wanted to work, I wouldn't steal for a living!"

"If you wanted to go through life easy, you should have

gotten a scholarship to Hamburger University."

"Don't you mean Clown College?"

"Same difference."

"How dark is it?"

"Dark enough to look at your face without screaming?"

"Any witnesses?"

"Nope, the place is ours."

"Good. Go ahead and put away the crayons. Grave rubbing is for pussies."

"Done."

"And get the shovels."

"Finally."

The circus drove us to drink, but Paul was better at this than me, just like most things, so when I say he was an alcoholic, I mean he was drinking straight-up poison like it was going out of style. Luckily, we were no longer concerned with style, or anything else respectable.

We were a couple of goddamn clowns, remember.

I was partial to ruining my life with beer, like a normal person, but Paul was drawn to the distinct plaid of that Luxco label, and the 190 Everclear grain alcohol wiggling its dick underneath that kilt. My only interaction with Everclear was that holy rite of passage—Purple Jesus: one bottle of Everclear and five packets of grape Kool-Aid. You bury it in an unused gas can for about three weeks, or however long the Bible said it took Jesus to rise again. Then you strain, serve, black out, and never, ever do that shit again.

Come to think of it, three weeks is about as long as I'm able keep Paul underground before someone's kicking open his coffin, but I'll get to that in a minute. Sorry, if you thought we lived through this.

But as far as steady work, we did a lot of birthday parties, sure, usually for free, though Paul was fond of saying, "It may be charity, but it's also a great sin," whatever that meant. And we also did our share of "Sweet Parties," too, of course, but there was always a carnival somewhere in Ohio, and they always needed clowns.

We were real popular. Paul especially. People swore he could make balloon animals that no sane man would ever attempt. Complicated structures. The Golden Gate Bridge, but while it was under construction? The Empire State Building, but during the last reel of King Kong? An anatomically accurate balloon model of the circulatory system of the Great White Shark, which was very similar to a human being's circulatory system, except for six distinct differences, or two balloons...

Yeah, he didn't do any of those. I did. That's how I got my nickname, actually, but Paul didn't mess with balloon animals at all. Some other clowns frowned on this, but, hell, those assholes were always frowning anyway. Their faces were drawn that way. But Paul always said the bubble in his brain was his only balloon animal, and one was enough for him. He said he could still hear it sometimes, stretching through his oblongata, squeaking and swelling and curling its rubbery tail until it runs the highway of veins, dead-ends and it runs out of room in that clown car of his skull and then POP!

No, I was Squeaky Pete, so I stuck to the balloons, and Fireball Paul just stuck to his fireballs. Busting out his Everclear and his lighter, and blowing fireballs so big and bright that the drunks would swear the sun had come up early. And whenever he lit his right arm on fire by mistake, we never felt a thing.

And at first glance, we were pretty similar, too. More similar than we ever were in school. Rainbow wigs, red rubber noses, blue-and-white polka dot jumpsuits, with three big silver buttons right down the middle. No need for the greasepaint these days. Clown faces got easier every year. Bank robberies had even made the full-head rigs popular, where you just slipped the entire clown face over your own grin, nose horn, Ronald McDonald eyebrows, and all. There was a reason clowns opted for easy costumes. It was really Einstein's famous habit of having ten suits, ties, and slacks always ready to roll every morning. Or maybe it was the guy from The Fly. Either way, why waste brain-power you could be using on clown-related mugging, or goofy knock-knock jokes, or intricate new balloon-animal constructions?

But one suit was really all we needed. You know, a lot has been written about a clown's big nose, big hair, those big-ass shoes. But people forget about the three buttons. It was those three big buttons that made a clown suit unusual, that made it recognizable from a distance, and it was Paul's buttons that made his suit even more unusual than that. Normally, we'd just have pom-poms down the middle where the buttons would be. But Fireball Paul had been peeled open once before by those big paramedic shears, so the silver buttons on his suit were kind of his trademark, because they were actually seven-inch platinum records. No bullshit.

He thought it would be funny if they were clown songs, of course. One of them was Smokey Robinson's "Tears of a Clown," The Every Brothers' "Cathy's Clown" and The Kink's "Death of a Clown."

I always thought "Stuck in the Middle with You" would be funnier, but it wasn't my jumpsuit. I pretended I didn't remember Michelle playing all those songs in rehab.

How did he get real platinum phonographs, you ask? Well, snagging a vacuum-coated metalized platinum 45 rpm record wasn't that big a deal. You could buy them for about a hundred bucks on eBay, depending on the song. The plaque they usually got framed with were sometimes worth more money than the record, depending on the artist, since they might be twenty-four-karat gold. Plus they're rarely the song you think they are. They typically dip any ol' record in gold just to be more efficient in the trophy factories. In fact, rumor has it Billy Joel got mad at Christie Brinkley and smashed his framed gold record of "Uptown Girl," and when they both calmed down, he put it on the record player to call a truce, but the song dipped in gold turned out to be Randy Newman's "Short People" instead. And you know what happened to them.

The point is, there were a lot of clowns in the world wearing goofy costumes, but those big silver buttons on Paul's suit added a touch of distinction, as well as a bit of history, and, as impossible as it may sound, a touch of class. It kept us both in demand anyway, steady work long after a clown would normally be too old to half-ass a kid's birthday party. He told his last stupid joke in the summer of '95, then died that same winter, a second bubble in his brain that popped and took the co-pilot of our clown car with it.

I thought about those bubbles in his brain a lot, even when I wasn't tying balloon knots, and decided that I was probably having them right along with him, only mine weren't fatal when they popped. But I was changing every time.

And even though I gave Nimbus so much grief for dwelling on his stroke like she did, I carried around his jumpsuit, too, folded up in my trunk with all the respect of an American flag. So it just seemed right to bury him in his suit.

The rumors started soon after, and maybe I started them. Who can tell? But what if his platinum records were really platinum? I mean, with platinum going at about $1,500 an ounce, that means almost fifty bucks a gram. So fifty times fifty times three. That's 7,500 bucks. Plus they say platinum is eleven percent denser than gold. So a record like that would weigh even more. Sure, I'm no mathematician, but I'm gonna go out on a limb and say that when we insisted on burying Fireball Paul in his suit, that clown might have been worth ten grand easy.

Unless it was just a rumor I'd started, of course. But true or not, we all still end up in a same place, am I right? Patrolling the final resting place of our dead and speaking when they can no longer speak for themselves.

I know what you're thinking. If the songs really went platinum, and if these are really platinum records, then they wouldn't be platinum. I'm not even following what the fuck I'm saying anymore, but the question is…is it really worth the effort? You know what I'm talking about.

Well, you'd be surprised. It turned out that quite a few people think it's worth a little effort, and worth a little digging. Unless you're not used to working for a living. But no one works harder than a clown.

"Did you know that typically when you're around the graves of famous people, there's a sign that warns of the penalties for defacing their tombstones."

"Fascinating."

"And because of this, every nearby headstone is covered in graffiti instead. As a kid, when the cops are trying to guilt you into not defiling graves anymore, you'll hear shit like, 'That was someone's brother, someone's son, someone's father, someone's grandfather…'"

"That's a good point."

"The problem with that argument is that the only thing you can be certain of is that it is someone's son. The other three are just guesses. And, honestly, who gives a fuck about someone else's son?"

"I sure don't."

"You should be ashamed of yourself."

"I am."

"Did you know that, besides Walmarts, the place most men masturbate is graveyards."

"No way."

"Yes. Way. It's because there are so many headstones at waist level. Way too easy to rub one out. And people will just think you're bowing your head to pay your respects."

"Do you think you'll enjoy hell?"

"Shut up. How much deeper do we have to go?"

"Until you hear his fucking nose honk."

"Wait, did you hear that?"

"Hear what?"

"Who's this guy in the trees…oh my God…"

"What the fuck is wrong with your face…"

POP! POP!

Looking at Fireball Paul's tombstone over the smoking barrels of my .45, I suddenly noticed the erratic motion of insects along the edges, even though it was much too cold for them. A swarm of black and blue flies have congregated around a tipped can of orange soda, occasionally dipping furry toes and noses in the sticky orange pool around the rim. I picked up the can and checked my reflection. What did they mean about my face? I guess it's like our mother always warned us. Don't grimace too long or your mouth will stay that way.

Did they say they were grave robbers or grave rubbers? Doesn't matter. No one would miss either one. I threw the can over my shoulder, and the flies stayed with me. I'm always amazed at what the cemetery crew doesn't clean up these days if they assume it's some sort of tribute. But what does a can of orange pop have to do with a dead clown? You could put an empty toilet-paper tube on a tombstone and forget the flowers and someone would hesitate to throw it away. So it's good I'm out here to help out.

I jumped down into the loose soil. The two grave robbers had gotten further than most, but it didn't matter. I'd dug up my better half so many times, I could do it in my sleep, and probably do. I liked their shovels though, and I kept the one with the price tag still on it. You get to appreciate a good shovel when you spend your weekends digging up and digging down.

When I hit Paul's casket, the lid was riding real high, like the top slice of a bulging club sandwich. Only this sandwich had arms and legs spilling out the sides instead of lettuce and tomato. And when I cleared enough dirt to swing the lid open, I saw the casket was way past capacity. But it's always been past capacity.

With Paul down there on the bottom, buried under too many treasure-seekers to count. None of this mattered. They'd fit. They'd always fit, and I could do this forever.

Lightning flashed as I stuffed the two new bodies on top. I tossed their grave rubbings over their chests, and I let the rain fill their surprised mouths for a full minute before I swung the lid back over their mugs, then I started to shovel the dirt in again, racing the first splash of sunrise on the horizon. There were so many bodies, it was getting quicker to refill, but I wasn't worried. His grave would never really be full. I knew this because Paul had told me the secret of a clown car the first time I dug him up. He'd lied about the trap door in the stage, you see.

"You want to know how they really pile so many clowns into those tiny cars?" he whispered as I played the silver record on his chest with my dirt-caked fingernail riding the groove.

"The trick is that they pile on in, but it doesn't matter if they ever pile on out."

STEALING SUNSHINE
Jeffery Hess

Fort Myers, Florida—August 14, 1987

After three hours twisting balloon animals for kids at the grand opening of Brennan's Ice Cream Parlor, all Sunshine the Clown had left in her canvas bag were her street clothes, a bottle of baby oil, some paper towels, a squeaky horn, and her Beretta 9mm pistol.

As the line outside grew, she snuck a look at Granny Brennan raking in another wad of cash at the register. Less than an hour to go until closing time.

Cold.

Sunshine felt cold air on her face. They kept the place freezing, but she stayed warm beneath her yellow polka-dot costume, pink wig, blue bowler hat with SUNSHINE THE CLOWN written across a cardboard sun stitched to the front, and white gloves left over from her Marine Corps dress blue uniform. To this day, she was only a dozen pounds over a hundred, but in costume everyone assumed she was bigger and younger and that made it easier to do her thing. The gloves worked equally well to tie balloons off and twist them to hand out, and kept her fingerprints off everything.

The place had checkerboard floors, pictures of celebrities

from the 1950s lined the walls along with 45 RPM records.

Sunshine opened the wooden ring handles of her bag, which had a bright orange sun and golden rays of light painted on both sides, and looked inside. Out of fucking balloons. She grabbed the squeaky horn, closed the bag and slid the rings over her arm.

Her floppy shoes were rubberized attachments to her regular shoes and she flop-flopped in them at about half her normal walking speed, with high knee kicks to allow the droopy toes to clear the floor with each step. Sudden turns or pivots were when she was likely to trip over the added length of each foot as she danced to the beat of her honked horn. Her pink wig and blue hat did much of the movement until she feared her neck would snap.

Sunshine's real name was Natalia, after her grandmother, and lately she'd needed some time away from Miami. She'd headed northwest, predicting some people might be looking for her on the East Coast. While they might've raced up I-95, she had chugged along Alligator Alley and up US-41 on the other side of the state. She'd stopped to get gas in Fort Myers. As she'd filled her tank, two guys had strung vinyl flags around the strip mall parking lot across the street.

She'd put on her makeup and costume in the gas station bathroom and driven over, introduced herself and talked her way into the gig. Her plan was to wait for the last customer to leave and then wave the Beretta around and take the day's till.

She wasn't proud. It was a tough existence, living on con jobs and robberies, but this life was no harder than a legit job on the rat wheel. She believed mind and body only thrived as long as they were challenged. She estimated as long as she didn't get scared or soft, she'd sail along until her enemies or her vices wiped her out, whichever came first.

Sunshine posed with anyone who wanted a picture. She made a production out of each pose as a way to fill the time, confident the white face paint, red mouth and nose would make it impossible for anyone to identify her. Good luck with my police sketch, she thought as she honked her horn and made faces at laughing children.

Through the plate glass window beside the entrance, a pale green pickup truck caught her attention as it screeched to a halt. She checked the clock. There were only thirty-seven minutes to go.

The door burst open and a man stormed in.

Her first instinct was to grab her pistol, but the man walked right up to her and grabbed her arm.

He was over six feet tall. Broad-shouldered, with thick arms straining the short sleeves of a red polo shirt. "I need you to come with me, Sunshine the Clown," he said. "I'll explain later."

She'd been trained to resist and reverse, but a shootout was in no one's best interest. She focused all her intensity onto the guy with his arm clamped across her throat and a gun in his hand.

"It's okay," the guy called out to the crowd in line and those seated with their ice cream. "I'm a bounty hunter and this is an escaped fugitive. I have it all under control." He held up his pistol and wallet.

She imagined it was happening too fast for the ice cream eaters to question, but it was a thing of beauty to watch. He was the type of guy who'd never experienced a moment of hesitation or doubt.

"I'll take it from here," he said at full volume. "You good people just go back to your sundaes and banana splits." He shoved her toward the door.

She walked slowly in her big shoes.

The guy was forceful. One hand clamped onto the back of her neck and the other twisted her wrist behind her. Despite the hoop in her clown suit, he applied pressure and steered her. He eased up the less she struggled. "I'm awfully sorry about this," he whispered in her ear.

She looked back at him. Had a few guesses what this was about. None of them good.

A gray-haired man with suspenders and wire-rimmed glasses held the door open for them.

Once they crossed the threshold, the so-called bounty hunter rushed her the distance to the green pickup truck with faded paint and mag wheels that sat idling.

The vinyl flags strung across the parking lot popped in the wind. Each sound could've been the revolver he held or the pistol in her bag, but she reminded herself it was just the wind.

"Get in," he commanded. As he guided her head into the truck, his voice softened as he said, "And watch your coconut."

The surprise of his word choice made Natalia twist her neck in his direction as he guided her in.

"Slide over and don't do anything stupid."

It smelled like vodka and German mustard. The keys jangled as her knee brushed past them hanging from the ignition. Her hoop filled the space.

He followed her in and pushed to get her costume out of his way so he could settle into position. The truck backfired as he floored the gas pedal.

Her stomach rose to her throat and pressed on her lungs. Her jaw clenched until the red clown makeup on her lips got slick from the friction. She tugged the wooden handles on her bag, confident she could get to her pistol quickly. She pulled at the puffy collar of her clown suit to get more breathing room.

"Who sent you?" she asked, her voice flat and calm.

The guy shrugged both hands off the wheel. "Who sent me?"

"If it's the Lopez brothers, man, we can work this out." She positioned her bag to slip her hand between the handles, past her jean shorts and blouse, over one of her sandals, and onto the grip of her 9mm.

The guy squeezed the wheel, ten and two, and shook his head. "It's not them," he said. "Not anybody."

"You some kind of pervert?" Natalia asked.

"Not hardly. I just need a few minutes of your time."

"You mean you grabbed me because I'm a clown?"

The question puzzled him for a second. "Why else would I abduct a clown?"

The relief on her skin worked its way from her pelvic floor to her chest. She reached out and clapped the seat between them. "So, this is like a clown emergency?"

His eyebrows arched in surprise that was tough to fake. He nodded and relaxed his grip on the wheel. "Yeah," he said, looking at her for an instant and then eyes back to the road. "That's exactly what it is."

"How'd you find me?

"Been driving around. Looking. Saw the plastic streamers or whatever they are. And there you were."

"Lucky me," she said as the stranglehold around her ribs and neck relented. Her slick lips parted as she exhaled. "Well," she said, pulling off the floppy shoe attachments, "I'm not doing shit until you tell me who you are and where we're going." She stuffed the floppy shoes into the bag.

"Damn it, clown. I've already apologized as nice as I can. If you don't accept it, that's your business. But trust me, options are slim and time is short."

Those lines changed the flow within her body. Her anger drifted out like surf on a sandy beach. It roared back as a rip curl of curiosity. She settled into the seat as much as she could with the costume's hoop.

"And, needless to say, I'll compensate you for your time."

She looked out her window. Cleared her throat. Waited a second and then turned back to him. If they were standing, she'd hug him. He looked like he gave good hugs.

"How much?" she asked.

"A hundred."

"Bullshit." She laughed and looked out her window. "A thousand!"

"You crazy?" he asked without turning toward her. "Two hundred."

"A thousand is the least I would've made tonight if not for you," she said to the glass between her and the wind.

"Yeah, if you robbed the place."

"Exactly," she said.

"You should thank me then." He looked at her and then eyes back on the road. "I'm pretty sure I just saved you from getting busted."

Heat surged to the top of her head. Her ears felt as if they might fry clean off. "Bullshit."

"Even if you did get the money," he said, "how were you going to put distance between you and them, and get out of that costume?"

He was right. Her car was parked in the same lot. Until then, she'd never realized they could follow her out and get her license plate number. She had no idea how to make a car disappear.

He slapped the wheel with the butt of his hand. "Why couldn't you be a normal clown?"

He drove west. Signs along the main road referenced Ft. Myers Beach, Sanibel, and Captiva.

She looked for a street sign, saw Estero Boulevard, and felt better being grounded at least that much.

The darkened beach peeked out between stilt houses, cinderblock motels, and dozens of construction sites building taller hotels and condos like everywhere else in Florida. It wasn't the highest-end beach she'd seen, but it wasn't the worst either. All this concrete would change it forever.

After a number of bends in the road, he turned into a driveway of crushed shells and parked between the pillars of a stilt house directly on the beach. In front of the truck, grassy dunes framed a path leading to the water. From the corner of her eye, she caught movement of him shoving his revolver into the foam of his seat between his legs.

He killed the lights and made the beach go black.

"This where you live?" she asked.

"Mind your business," he said. "Just do your thing and I'll drive you back."

He held her arm, but didn't squeeze or tug her. The rustle of gulf waters lapped at the coarse sand. He looked cool in a real and raw way without having to pretend. Big and handsome. Thick hair. Thick arms. She followed his V-shaped torso up a stairway overhung by once-manicured vines and into the house.

The front door opened to a living room with a fireplace and couches and a desk with a green-shaded lamp in the far corner. There were hallways in either direction and a few doors.

"This doesn't look like much of a party," she said.

"Come with me." He held her by the arm.

"Wait." She opened her sunshine bag, dug in, and pulled out the floppy shoe attachments. "If we're doing this, got to do it right."

The rest of the walk down the short hallway went slower as a result.

He pulled her by the arm like a hunter dragging home his prey.

"I'll make sure she's up to it first. When I whistle, that's your cue."

He opened the door at the end of the hall.

The room smelled of ammonia and was dark except for a couple of decorative lights over the nightstands hanging by shiny chains hooked to the ceiling. Amber light glowed from fixtures designed to look like gemstones. A woman sat in bed, propped on a stack of pillows.

Natalia stayed in the doorway as he walked in and moved away the rolling tray table with an untouched cube of green Jell-O on a white saucer.

He fluffed an extra pillow and placed it amongst the existing stack so her head was higher. The whistle came in two soft bursts, as if musical notes that meant, "Come now."

It was showtime.

Natalia dropped into a pratfall and continued into a summersault and stuck the landing between the door and the bed. She'd always taken her coordination and athleticism for granted, until now. She stared at the woman in the bed. A woman so obviously close to the end that it made Natalia feel bigger, stronger, and even younger.

It wasn't a hospital bed, but there was a wheelchair and an aluminum frame walker, and the tray table with the Jell-O was on wheels that slid under the bed. A bedpan ready on the nightstand.

"Denise, honey," the guy said in a voice even kinder than when he'd apologized earlier. "This is Sunshine the Clown."

The frail figure barely dented the sheets. Natalia recognized what was once an attractive face, now too thin to tell what was age and what was disease. The guy held her hand and rocked.

Natalia almost wished she had balloons left in her bag.

Instead, she removed her blue hat and waved it widely as she curtsied.

The nightstand had orange pill bottles, a pitcher of water, and a framed picture of the two of them standing in front of Cinderella's castle at Disney World. The TV was on, but the sound was off.

Sunshine the Clown rose to stand and then dropped into a backward somersault. All she had was the clown horn and those floppy shoes and she played it all just as she had in the ice cream shop. High-stepping, duckwalking, and honk, honk, honking.

She performed not for the sick woman, but for him. She had his attention and worked harder to impress him. It wasn't the weirdest way she'd earned a buck, but it made her top ten.

In the transition between high-step and duckwalk, she studied their faces in blinks like camera shots. There was pleasure there, so she continued and then repeated. Honking the honking honk.

The only pause in their happiness was the split second the

guy wiped the woman's chin with a handkerchief retrieved from beneath her pillows.

"Thank you," he said as Natalia took a series of bows for dramatic effect, milking each one and looking at him on every downswing. "I'll meet you in the living room," he said.

As polite a dismissal as it was, she was almost sorry the performance was over. She flopped her floppy shoes across the carpet and she honked her horn once more. By the time she got to the door, she decided it was just beginning.

Natalia left the sickroom with sweat rolling from every pore. She kicked off her shoes with the floppy extensions attached and reached behind her neck to grab the zipper. She tugged twice to get it started then repositioned her arm to slide it all the way down. The flood of cold air felt good enough to electrify her skin. She peeled the costume off her shoulders and stepped out of the hoop insert. Next came the hat and the pink wig, which she tossed onto the sofa.

She stood barefoot in underwear she'd seen in the window of Frederick's of Hollywood at the mall. Royal blue and cut perfectly to obscure just the most private parts. She kept her gloves on and used them to rake through her hair. She heard the sickroom door open and close. Her heartbeat stayed constant until he walked into the living room.

"Hey," he said, looking directly at her. "Thank you for what you did in there."

His focus gave her a sensation. She felt the tingle in her armpits and underneath her toes.

"Worked up a sweat doing it. It's hot as a bitch in this thing," she said, wadding up the costume. "I needed to feel some A-C on my A-S-S."

He didn't laugh. He didn't turn away.

The panties were cut high on her hips, which she kept shapely by maintaining her PT schedule of running and weight training.

She liked her tits. Liked everything about her body except the oblong belly button, which she covered with her right hand.

Despite her lack of modesty, she was happy to have the clown makeup. There was power in remaining anonymous. There was also something tantalizing about withholding one thing that she was offering him.

"Just a little different than the pear-shaped silhouette of the clown suit, huh?" she said.

"What's your name?" he asked.

She sidled up to him, her slightly covered hipbone less than an inch from his thigh. She swore she could feel the heat. "You never told me your name."

He stepped away to open a cabinet door as if to find something. "My name is Steve."

She put her hands on her tanned hips. "It fits you." She walked around the coffee table and stood within inches of him again.

He stood a foot taller. The top of her head came to his shoulder. Her lips were perfect height for his sternum. She wanted to put her mouth there and taste his salt, but he folded an old newspaper and stuffed it in a magazine rack. She raised on her bare toes and closed the distance. Her hand reached the valley between his chest muscles and she traced a finger down to rest on his belt buckle.

His deep stare switched to a lack of eye contact. He seemed to look at everything else in the room. He opened and closed his mouth twice as if to speak, but chose not to. He leaned his head back. His face tensed. Pelvis pushed toward her hand. He half-smiled, dimpling just his right cheek. His breathing came faster and she watched his shirt tighten and loosen with each quick breath. He looked back at the sickroom door then into Natalia's eyes.

She ran a gloved fingernail up his leg. Up to the top. Grabbed him full. Felt him grow in her gloved hand.

His breathing came heavy, but at the same pace.

Tension in her legs grew tight. She squeezed her hand and

lightly bit his shoulder. She tingled all over. Got lightheaded from the shiver that shot through her.

The waves breaking outside and the crickets chirping and the smell of ammonia coming from the sickroom meant nothing compared to friction with his jeans that heated her hand. She wanted to touch skin.

He bit his lip and nodded. "It's been so long," he whispered.

"Where should we go?" she whispered as she squeezed.

"Right here," he said just before she kissed him.

Surprise and fireworks burst inside her. The kiss wasn't planned. She bit his lip, but he didn't pull away. He kissed back. Smeared her makeup on his nose and cheeks.

In mid-grope, she felt his hand on her shoulder. He pushed her back to arm's length, like a man who'd lost his appetite. He checked the sickroom door again, as if that woman could walk out of there and catch them. "No," he said with a mirror image of her red smile on his face. "It can't happen."

She raked a gloved hand through her hair then waved it in front of her face to fan herself. She took a deep breath and squeezed her toes on the area rug. "But she's—"

Blood rose to his face, made his head and ears turn red. He pointed a finger in her face. "You don't know a thing about her."

Natalia raised her chin. His tone reminded her of the drill instructor she'd had at Parris Island. "God damn it!" she said. "Can't you think about somebody besides yourself?"

He pointed. "Did you not see my dying wife in there?"

"Life is for the living." She smoothed the lace around her heavily pawed breast. "Now take me to bed in one of these other rooms."

He looked her up and down. Natalia watched his eyes travel from her bare feet to her makeup.

"To be honest with you," he said, "I can't imagine anything sexier right now, but nothing comes between me and that incapacitated woman."

Natalia couldn't force down the wad of jealousy in her throat.

"I'd run a marathon on broken glass if it could give her a minute's comfort," he said.

She walked over and picked up her hat and wig. "Not how I planned this day to go, at all."

He leaned with his hand on a wall, his thick back expanded with every deep breath. He turned and said, "I'll get you paid and drive you back. Let me just check on her first."

"Make it quick. I need to split." Natalia didn't bother telling him about the red smile smeared across his face.

The first doorway in the hall was a bathroom. She pulled the baby oil and paper towels from her bag and removed her makeup with the help of the mirror above the shell-shaped sink. She tossed the wadded paper towels into the plastic pail next to the toilet and walked back to the living room, cool tile beneath her bare feet. She pulled on her jean shorts, a red blouse, and sandals. In her own clothes with her own hair and face, as if being truly nude. Sunshine the Clown was just a memory. She held the same bag, but had turned it inside out so the clown advertising on the inside revealed a leopard print on the reverse. It wasn't her style, but she'd had to work with what she was given, or rather, had taken.

The sickroom door opened and closed with two different clicks.

She no longer had the makeup to hide behind. It was just her and his eyes were all over her.

"So, this is the real you."

"No, I'm a woman of a thousand disguises. Now give me my damn money already and let's get out of here. I've got shit to do."

He walked to the fireplace along the far wall, just past the bathroom she used to clean her face. The fireplace was stacked stone with a sharp white mantle and a knee-high hearth. He removed the copper fire screen to reveal a safe. He sat on the hearth and spun the dial too fast for her to get any numbers. As he pulled it open, she almost gasped out loud.

That's a beautiful pile of money, she thought.

"Well—" he peeled off ten one hundred dollar bills," —as I said, I appreciate your time."

The intensity boiling inside her became the rage-fueled anger she'd learned to channel in the Corps. The Corps is where she'd learned to discriminate between target and non-target. She reached into her bag, tugged on her gloves.

As he moved to close the safe, Natalia walked over, clicked the barrel of her pistol on the open door. "Hang on a second."

He sat back, the surprise on his face as obvious as the pistol in her gloved hand, but showed no signs of fear.

"Now why does a clown need a gun?" His voice held just the right amount of acknowledgment and sarcasm.

Natalia fell deeper in love with him. "Because it takes more than greasepaint and a wig to get the day's till." She dropped her leopard-print bag at his feet. "Since you didn't fill me up, you're going to fill up that bag."

His hand reached for the small of his back. He looked around the living room, his eyes expectant. It was quiet.

"Looking for your revolver?" she asked. "Don't bother. It's tucked into the driver's seat stuffing, right where you left it."

He didn't speak or indicate she was wrong. Instead, he sat with a look in his eye that conveyed he was confident he could spring off that hearth, take the gun from her, and reverse this scenario.

She tried to hide her fear, but without any makeup she had no idea if she was convincing.

He laughed.

She backed up a step and aimed her pistol. "I can put you down hard, but not permanent. You'll live, but it'll be ugly. Especially with a funeral to plan."

"You don't count these as extenuating circumstances? A time

like this?"

"A time like what? People die every day. So what? The more accurate point is I don't find free stacks of hundred-dollar bills every day."

"You're about the worst person I've ever met."

"You shouldn't have shown me your stash."

He swiped a hand over his face and his posture caved for the first time. He squeezed his eyes shut for a second or two. "My fault. I should've made you wait outside while I opened the safe. But I didn't. That's on me. I'm not exactly in my regular frame of mind. These days, I sleep at most two hours in a row."

Natalia nodded. "Tell you what," she said. "Keep a thousand for yourself."

He stood and propped a foot on the hearth. Leaned an elbow on his knee. He stayed like that longer than Natalia would've liked. It made her uncomfortable. Not the silence, but rather the fact that he was thinking things through.

"Okay, big man," she said. "How about you get your hand away from the fire poker."

He looked down at his fingers an inch away from the handle. He laughed. "That's just muscle memory."

He reached for it and Natalia squeezed off a round.

If the boom didn't shake the sick woman from that bed, nothing would. Natalia wagged her head to clear the ringing in her ears.

He sat hard on the hearth and checked his arm. It was little more than a friction burn. An even better shot than she'd hoped. Just to get his attention.

He held his hand over the wound and licked his lips, slow and drawn out. It made him look thoughtful.

She wanted to punish him for being a good man…and because she'd never have a man feel that way about her.

"Now, you can try and be a hero again," she said. "You might get me. Then again, I might get off another shot or two. You've seen how accurate I am. I can take out a kidney or hit your spinal cord or get you right in the heart. Just rest assured that I'll get that money and leave the door open on the way out so animals can get in and feast on your corpse." She pointed toward the bedroom. "Both your corpses."

His posture went rigid. His face locked up like a rock. He balled a fist and ground it into the palm of his other hand. His forearms seemed to swell with muscle and veins, sturdy jaw grinding back and forth.

"It's a shit position to be in," she said. "Not but one option for you."

He emptied the safe into her bag and stood. Tugged at the tightness of his polo shirt and applied direct pressure to his wound. "Go on then," he said.

Natalia picked up the bag, keeping the pistol aimed center of mass. "Now the keys to that piece of shit truck."

He dug into his pocket and pulled out a key ring with the green plastic triangle that had brushed her knee earlier.

She held out her hand, but he made her wait while he removed a key.

"Front door." He held up the lone key and tossed her the set.

She snatched them from the air. "Under different circumstances," she said, "we could've been good together."

"Get the fuck out before I change my mind," he said as he headed down the hall toward the sickroom.

Natalia started the truck and cried three short jags before locking down her emotions. She had to decide if she'd go back to Miami and pay off the Lopez brothers or resume her journey to party it up in Tampa. Neither seemed enjoyable now.

BAD BREAK
Lono Waiwaiole

I get the idea from Sidewinder, in spite of the fact that ideas aren't exactly that bull's claim to fame. He's a lot more famous for throwing cowboys like Jesse Johnson on their skinny butts in the dust, which is what he's doing when the idea hits me.

I don't have a chance to give it a lot of thought, though, because I have to go to work as soon as Jesse gets thrown—it's my job to make sure he doesn't come to any harm before the pickup riders can whisk him away to safety, which in this case is more than a little ironic.

What I have to do is make Sidewinder come after me instead of Jesse, which I know sounds like a crazy-ass thing to do. But it's great work if you can get it, you can take my word on that. I've been clowning rodeos for almost twenty years, and wouldn't trade the worst minute of it for whatever the fuck it is that you do. On the other hand, I would pay you good money to take the rest of my miserable life off my hands hook, line and sinker, which is why I'm open to suggestion when the idea from Sidewinder hits me.

Actually, that mean motherfucker hits me with more than an idea on my way into the barrel—the barrel being the only refuge we clowns have in an arena wide open all the way from one end to the other. Sidewinder does his level best to get at me even after I'm inside the thing, knocking me around until the pickup riders finally chase him off to the holding pens.

The crowd lets out a huge sigh of relief when I finally poke my head out of the barrel. I look around like I still fear for my life, which we immediately turn into a joke. That's the other part of my job—providing comic relief—explaining why I'm dressed like a clown instead of a cowboy.

"You can come on out now, Cactus Jack!" Jed says from the announcer's perch above all the action on the ground, talking from a script that we both know by heart.

"The fellas done run ol' Sidewinder off."

"Are you dead solid certain?" I say as soon as I get my microphone switched back on. "Fella cain't be too careful out here!"

"You don't see him, do you?"

"I couldn't see him when I was crouched down in this here barrel, neither, but that don't mean he wasn't out here!"

"Let's hear it for Cactus Jack!" Jed says as I climb out of the barrel into a wave of laughter, still looking around like it might be the biggest mistake of my life. "He just went toe to toe with ol' Sidewinder and is right back on his feet again!" I raise my arms and flex a couple of times while the applause rolls out of the grandstand, then I take one step and fall flat on my ass with both feet sticking straight up in the air. The part about the feet is key, of course, because that's how the folks know it's okay to laugh at my collapse.

And laugh they do, with Jed goading them on. "That ain't a-gonna work, Cactus Jack," he says. "You gotta get them big feet on the ground 'fore you can get anywheres."

I just let that simmer for a minute or two while I wiggle both feet in the air, then I roll straight up into a handstand and start walking around on my hands for a while. "I guess this shows how much you know!" I say as the crowd roars, but I have to cut it shorter than usual when I start to feel the blood trickling down my left forearm from the spot where Sidewinder hooked me.

That's the thing about blood—it isn't fucking funny at all,

which I'm going to prove to Jesse Johnson if it's the last thing I ever do.

Jesse had a good feeling about his draw as soon as he heard it was Sidewinder because a cowboy who knew what the fuck he was doing could ride that son of a bitch. The bull was twisty as hell (hence the name) but predictable—he spun to the right immediately after clearing the chute and didn't quit spinning until either the rider was gone or eight seconds had transpired, whichever came first.

That's why Jesse was leaning the wrong way from the jump and was airborne as soon as Sidewinder spun to the left. Where the fuck did that come from? he said to himself as he hit the ground not more than a yard or two in front of a bull apparently pissed off about Jesse invading his private space in the first place.

Sidewinder lowered his head and started to charge, leaving Jesse kissing his sorry ass goodbye until Cactus Jack flew in out of nowhere. Fool is fast for an old fucker, I'll give him that, Jesse thought as he crab-walked backwards while the bull and the clown went nose to nose for a minute. Next thing he knew, he was up behind a pickup rider and Cactus Jack was racing for the barrel like his life depended on getting there before Sidewinder caught him.

"Damn!" he said as Cactus Jack disappeared from sight. "Have to admit that motherfucker's good, don't I?"

"Most people wouldn't have to strain themselves to do it," the rider said as they cleared the gate and Jesse slipped to the ground.

"Most people don't hate his fuckin' guts, Rowdy."

"Whatever," Rowdy said before he rode off toward the trailers without another word.

What the fuck is stuck in his craw? Jesse wondered, and he was still working with that thought when he got to the cluster of cowboys lounging along the arena fence.

"Tough break, JJ," Wilson said. "Ain't never seen Sidewinder go left like that before."

No shit, Jesse said to himself rather than Wilson in hopes of cutting the conversation short, but the gambit was no more successful than his attempt to ride Sidewinder had been.

"Cactus Jack was sure as hell in good form, though," Wilson said next. "That shit he pulled out there this time was classic."

"Tell me about it," Jesse said, although he regretted his choice of words immediately. That fool is the last subject in the world I would choose to be told about, he thought as he walked off toward the woman leaning with her fine backside against the fence and her black eyes locked on every step he took.

"Tell me, Jed," I say while the crew sets up for the barrel racers and we have some time to kill. "You wanna hear a knock-knock joke?"

"That depends, Cactus Jack," Jed says.

"Depends on what?"

"Depends on whether it's funny or not."

"Well, of course it's funny. That's what makes it a joke!"

"I hate to be the one to point this out, but in seventeen years of working rodeos together I have yet to hear you tell a single funny joke."

"Well, I guaran-damn-tee you this one is funny. But you're right about one thing."

"What one thing is that?"

"It ain't gonna sound funny to you."

"Why in the world wouldn't a funny joke sound funny to me?"

"'Cause it's gonna bare-ass you."

"It's gonna do what?"

"It's gonna bare-ass you."

"I think the word you're lookin' for there is embarrass, Cactus Jack."

"That's what I just said—it's gonna bare-ass you."

"Just how in the world is it gonna do that?"

"Well, it's gonna prove that even after seventeen years workin' with all the top cowboys in the world, you still don' know the first thing about cows."

"That could be the craziest thing I've ever heard! I reckon I know just about everything there is to know on the subject of cows."

"It ain't so crazy that I cain't prove it, though."

"That I'd like to hear!"

"No, sir, you would not. Nobody likes to be bare-assed, believe me."

"What I believe is you're stallin' here, Cactus Jack."

"Are you absolutely sure you wanna hear this?"

"I am absolutely sure."

"Okay, here we go! Oh, wait a minute. You have to know how a knock-knock joke works first."

"Everybody here knows how a knock-knock joke works. You gonna quit your stallin' or not?"

"Fine. Just don't say after it's done that I didn't warn you! Knock knock!"

"Who's there?"

"Cows say."

"Cows say who?"

"No, they don't," I say. "I bet everyone here today but you knows cows say moo!"

This draws a loud laugh from the crowd just like it always does, but I don't share in it at all—I'm already back in my head to the idea I got from Sidewinder.

"That couldn't have been much fun," Marisol said when Jesse got within range of a whisper.

"You can say that again," Jesse said.

"That couldn't have been much fun."

Jesse almost cracked a smile in response to that, but not quite. "Why do you always do that?"

"Because you ask me to, of course. You might have noticed that I do pretty much everything you ask me to do."

"Except the main thing."

"The main thing is not that easy, Jesse. I owe him."

"You ain't never owed him as much as you've given him already."

Marisol didn't speak again for a while and neither did Jesse, and when the silence ended he missed it immediately. "Maybe," Marisol said finally, "but it's sure as shit more than I owe you."

I haven't got a death wish no matter what you might think of my line of work, which is why I haven't yet done a thing about Jesse and Marisol. It isn't that I don't know what has to be done, it's just that I don't know how to get away with doing it.

Or I didn't know until Sidewinder showed me the way, which is why I need a whole new look at the situation now. I knew about it almost from the git-go, of course—I could feel the change in her, and a blind man could have seen it in him. And it's not like I blame her for it, either, or didn't expect it to happen at some point. She doesn't deserve to be saddled with an old coot like me forever, and I can honestly say I'm fully prepared to accept a change something like this one. But with Jesse Johnson, who's been plowing furrows all the way from Calgary to California and back again? No fucking way in hell.

"Has he said anything to you?" Jesse asked from his side of the truck. He was parked in the slot farthest from the door of the club, but he knew it wasn't as far away as they needed to be.

"No," Marisol said, her eyes turned toward the nothing out the window next to her rather than at him.

"What makes you think he knows, then?"

"Everybody knows, Jesse. Why wouldn't he?"

"Seems like he'd say somethin'. It was me, I sure the fuck would."

Marisol turned her head slowly in Jesse's direction and studied him for a moment. "He isn't you, though, is he?" she said when the moment ended.

I don't need all this fuckin' attitude, Jesse thought, but what he said was this: "That's why you're here, isn't it?"

"Yes," she said after another silent moment. "But that doesn't mean I'm proud of it."

"Look, you don't want to do this, then don't do it."

"Wouldn't really bother you, would it?"

"Don't try to make this about me. You're the one can't seem to make the obvious move here."

"Yeah," Marisol said softly, her eyes glowing wetly in the shadow on her side of the truck. "That's exactly who I am."

What I got from Sidewinder is a lot easier to identify than to implement, but I start the process at The Lariat as soon as the evening show is over. Every table in the club is occupied, but Marisol is one of the occupants and the seat across from her is waiting for me. I wander through the throng in her direction, but I'm looking around for Jesse.

I finally see him in a crowd of cowboys leaning with his back against the bar, and he's staring directly back at me with a beer in his hand. He raises the glass in my direction and I nod in acknowledgement, I know it has something to do with our shared experience with Sidewinder, but I don't stretch the moment out and neither does he. I focus instead on Marisol, and a moment later I'm sitting across the table from her.

"Hey," I say.

"Back atcha," she says as she leans in my direction. Her soft red lips are leading the way, and I go to meet them in the middle. We kiss, and she looks up at me as soon as we separate with an expression that only the most fortunate of men ever see on a woman's face.

"Did you see the matinee today?" I ask, even though I know she watches them all.

"Cactus Jack outdid himself," she says. "Everyone's talkin' about it."

"Everyone's always talking about something."

"Yeah," she says softly, and her eyes dim like she just walked into a cloudbank.

"We both knew this time was going to come," I say as I reach across the table and take her right hand in both of mine. "I was too old for you ten years ago."

"How long have you known?"

"I think from the beginning."

"Why didn't you say something?"

"Probably the same reason you didn't. We weren't quite ready yet, were we?"

"And now?"

"I think so."

"I know you don't like him."

"I wouldn't have liked whoever it turned out to be. If he's the one scratches where you itch, I say go for it."

"Doesn't sound very pretty if you put it like that, does it?"

It is what it is, Marisol, I say to myself. "That was uncalled for," I say to her. "I guess I'm not quite as civilized about this as I want to be."

"You're a lot more civilized than he would be in the same situation."

Or not, I say, but there is not a single decibel behind my voice so she doesn't hear either word.

"I don't believe it," Jesse said from the seat across from Marisol that the fucking clown had recently abandoned.

"Of course you don't," Marisol said.

"What's that supposed to mean?"

"It's not supposed to mean anything."

"Fuck it isn't. This seems to be a constant theme of yours lately, and I don't like it."

"Look, he knows, we talked, he's accepting it. What is it that you don't like about all that?"

Nothing, Jesse thought. I like all that just fine. "I guess I've been expecting a totally different kind of reaction," he said, and then he waited for her to say "Of course you did."

She didn't say that, though, or anything else. What she did instead was lean across the table and kiss him with the kind of heat that had drawn him toward her in the first place. "I feel free to be with you now," she said when she finally drew back to her side of the table. "That is important for me."

"I know," Jesse said before he tacked on a lie he knew she would like. "It's important for me, too."

"You ready to take me somewhere else, cowboy?"

"I'm ready to take you right here," he said with the same grin on his face that had worked like magic on a wide assortment of willing partners before this one.

"But I can wait if somewhere else ain't too fuckin' far from here."

I watch them get up and head for the exit from the spot at the bar recently held down by Jesse, Marisol holding on to Jesse's arm as they work their way through the throng.

"You seem to be takin' this pretty well," Rowdy says from the spot next to me.

"I was too old for her from the git-go," I say. "I wish her nothing but the best."

"I don't believe I could do the same in the same situation."

"Of course," I say through a slight chuckle, "you never got the chance to be in the same situation, did you?"

"Not for lack of tryin', believe me."

That I do believe, my friend, I think. That girl disappointed a whole shitload of you sorry motherfuckers when she decided to go with me. "The thing is," I say, "me and her never did make any sense."

"No shit."

"That's why it's hard to be anything but grateful at this point."

"I guess," Rowdy said with a shake of his head. "But I hate to see her with that asshole."

Now it's my turn to say "no shit," but I don't do it because it doesn't advance my effort to tamp down my obvious motive for malice. What I do say is this: "Rowdy, let me know when you come across a woman that you understand. I'd like to see what a creature like that looks like."

"I can try to do that," he says. "But I was you, I wouldn't hold my fuckin' breath."

"Don't worry about it," Marisol said.

"Easy for you to say," Jesse replied from his side of the bed, his eyes fixed on the naked ceiling above them rather than on the useless appendage between his legs.

"Yes, it is."

"It's not the same thing for a woman."

"No, it isn't," she said, rolling up against his shoulder and leaning in to kiss the side of his nose. "That's why you shouldn't worry about it."

"Get the fuck off me, girl," he said as he turned away from her lips. "When I want you, you'll know it."

"Stop it, Jesse. We both know you'll be fine as soon as you get a decent ride."

Jesse did know that, but he was a little surprised that Marisol shared that knowledge. "Please," she said as though reading his mind. "I've been around this life since the day I was born. I know everything there is to know about you fucking cowboys."

Or the non-fucking cowboys, apparently, he thought. "Do you know you're too good for me?" he said, actually agreeing with the thought for a moment.

"Absolutely," she said softly, moving in for another run at the side of his nose and hitting the target this time. "But I'm stuck with your sorry ass anyway."

"Yes, you are," he said, turning in so he could line his lips up with hers. He kissed her then, but his mind wasn't on it and she knew that, too. What they were both thinking instead was Jesse hadn't finished in the money for a month—not since before Sidewinder three rodeos ago—and that he was up on a bull the next day that always gave a cowboy a good run.

I'm more than ready when Jesse comes out on Terminator opening night in Pendleton, but I've been primed to follow Sidewinder's example for almost half of the season by now. After a solid eight seconds go by, Jesse tries to jump clear and can't do it—his hand gets caught in his rigging and Terminator soon has him flopping like a fish on a line.

I wrap one arm around Jesse as soon as I get there and go for the rigging with my free hand, but Terminator tosses us both around for a while before I shake Jesse loose. Which is when I finally get my chance to do the opposite of what is expected—instead of pulling Jesse clear with me, I drag both of us directly under the bull.

Terminator turns out to have five or six feet rather than four, and I do my best to keep us both under all of them for as long as I can. We start with Jesse on top and me on the bottom, me with both arms around Jesse now and holding him close. He tries to wriggle away but I don't let him, and after a sweet moment or two I roll us over and pin him under me while I take the brunt of those flying feet for a while.

The pickup riders finally get Terminator off of us, but neither of us jumps back on our feet. I don't do it because I'm leaning over to check on Jesse instead, and he's not doing it because he can't.

"Leave me the fuck alone," Jesse said. He was sprawled out on his back with his face turned toward the white wall on his left, Marisol seated in a straight-backed chair on the opposite side of the bed.

"No," she said.

"I don't want you here."

"Yes, you do."

"I broke my fucking back, Marisol, not my brain. I know what the fuck I want."

"Whatever," she said as she leaned over him and planted a kiss on his cheek.

"When you can throw me out of the room, cowboy, go ahead and do it. Until then, your sorry butt belongs to me."

"What's the word?" Marisol says as she walks into my room. I'm beat up pretty good and have one leg in a cast, but I really have only one complaint at the moment.

"This fuckin' thing itches already," I say.

"That's five words," she says as she leans in on me and plants a soft kiss on my forehead.

"How about Jesse?" I say.

"He might never walk again," she says, her dark eyes suddenly wet.

How sweet it is, I think. "I'm really sorry," I lie as I wrap my arms around her and draw her close. How sweet this is, too, I say where she can't hear it.

"You did as much as you possibly could, Robby."

I tried to do a helluva lot more, I think. "It doesn't feel that way," I say.

"Cactus Jack saved Jesse's life," she says, "at the risk of his own. You know that, right?"

"I guess."

"Ask anyone. You don't have to take my word for it."

"I know what everyone's saying. It's just hard to feel good about it with Jesse laid up like he is."

"I'm just thankful you were the one out there when it happened," she says, stepping back a little to look into my eyes. "He couldn't have been in better hands."

My feelings exactly, I think, but what I ask is this: "So now what?"

"Now I do whatever I can for him for as long as he lets me," she says, her voice barely above a whisper. "It's for better and for worse, right?"

These are not the words I'm hoping to hear, and they poke a hole in my resolve to be nice. "I think that's part of a marriage vow, Mar."

"Same same," she says with a shake of her head. "Marriage is just a word."

"Look, you don't owe him the rest of your life because of this."

"It's not because of this. You know how I am."

"I know how you were," I say, the words riding on a bitter edge that I know she can hear. "I don't know exactly what to think of you now, to tell you the truth."

"This is different, Robby."

"If you say so."

"You never really needed me, did you?"

"And you thought Jesse did?" I say through a brittle laugh.

"No," she says, her wet eyes finally overflowing. "It was me that needed something at first. But he sure does need me now, doesn't he?"

"I know what you did, motherfucker," Jesse said. He was flat on his back staring daggers at the man on crutches just inside the door to his room.

"You mean when I saved your sorry ass?" Robby said.

"Fuck Cactus Jack and the clown car he rode in on."

"You did. Turns out his rodeo days are over, too."

"Imagine my regret and sorrow. What the fuck are you doing here, anyway?"

"I thought I should offer my congratulations. You won, you know."

"Says the guy up and walking around."

"I got the edge there, no doubt. But you won the girl."

"Yeah," Jesse said as he turned his face toward the wall. "Now that I can't stand the sight of her, she's all mine."

"Reminds you of what you can't do anymore, does she?"

"Fuck you, Robby."

"And I can tell you from several years of personal experience, it will be a while before you can run her off."

"Next time you stick your head in my door, I'll be prepared to blow it the fuck off."

"I don't think I'll need to come back," Robby said through a twisted grin. "This wasn't the outcome I was hoping for, but it ain't half bad."

THE PARTY
Jen Conley

What he noticed first was the steep, long, wooden staircase. It led up to a small deck and a door to the side of the boxy, large house set on an incline. A ghostly light glowed under the deck's overhang. This was the way inside.

Matt stood on the road, locking his car. "Looks like *The Exorcist* in the woods." The shadows of tall trees loomed around them.

Dina came round and hooked her arm through his. The night was cold, icy, but she was still wearing her spiky boots. "Your mind goes to the weirdest places," she said, smiling. They'd been seeing each other since they met at a bar in early December. Dina had been out with her co-workers, he'd stopped in for a couple drinks by himself. "Hey," she'd said to him when he'd come in from a cigarette. She was petite and cute, recently divorced with no kids, and before he knew it, she was sitting next to him, and they were in deep into conversation. By the end of the week, they were a thing. Coming up to Connecticut was important to her, even in February. "They're my oldest friends and I want them to meet you." The friends owned the house. The rest of the people were neighbors or people they knew from their kids' soccer practice and the like.

"Careful," he said as they cautiously hiked along the slippery driveway, approaching the staircase. Matt noticed a sidewalk to the right, swirling up to a real front door but it appeared that was the wrong entry. It was a strange house. Part split level, part New England Colonial.

"They should salt this," Matt said as they climbed the stairs.

"This is Connecticut, baby. They're used to this weather."

It was a long climb, about twenty steps until they reached the deck. Dina led the way to the side door and they quickly left the quiet night, entering into a narrow mud room which opened to a kitchen buzzing with noise. People, holding their drink glasses or bottles of beer, turned around and looked, smiled, waved. The kitchen island, made of cream-colored marble, glimmered under the shine of hanging pewter lamps. The house was open-concept and to the left a large, long table was filled with food, probably appetizers. A thin woman with wild red hair rushed over, calling out, "Dina! So glad you came!" They hugged and then a bald man in a loose collared shirt put his beer down on the island and followed up with another hug. These were the owners of the house: Wendy and Colin. Wendy had been Dina's college roommate at Montclair University.

"Is this him?" Wendy said, quickly embracing Matt, pulling him close. Her wild hair smelled like hair product and indoor cooking. "Welcome. I've heard so much about you," she said.

Colin shook Matt's hand. "What beer are you drinking?" He patted him on the back and brought him over to a stainless steel cooler on a side table in the living room.

The house was hot and loud. The Beatles were playing from a Bose sound system and people sat on couches or stood in groups, welcoming Matt as Colin took him around.

"Dina's guy," he said and everyone nodded approvingly. "From Jersey."

"Giants or Eagles?" one man asked and Matt said, "Jets."

The men laughed.

Colin led Matt around the house, pointing out the bathroom they just had refinished and the Gaelic art piece they'd bought in Ireland. "Have you been?"

Matt had never been out of the country.

"You gotta go."

They went upstairs to the bedrooms, Colin pointing out his son's room, then his daughter's, then the master, and then the extra room. He took him all the way down to the bottom floor, a basement if it had been underground but it wasn't. The strange house was built on an incline after all, hence the sinister steps to the side of the house. Several kids lazed on three couches, the little kids draped over the couch arms or on the floor, all focused while two boys played a video game on a large flat screen TV. A coffee table held bowls of chips and carrot sticks and dip.

"We hide them down here when we have these things," Colin whispered.

"Like *Chitty-Chitty Bang Bang*," Matt said.

It took a quick second before Colin slapped him on the back and howled. "That's right! I forgot about that movie."

Matt was good with movies—it was his thing. "Dad, Dad," his son Jake used to call when Jeopardy was on. "Horror movie category!" Just the passing thought of those times choked Matt's heart. Being around these sequestered kids didn't help.

He needed a cigarette but had promised Dina he would wait at least an hour before venturing outside. "Let people get alcohol in them," she'd said at the hotel. "They'll be less judgey and less likely to lecture you when you come back in."

"Stinking of smoke?" Matt said.

"You should quit, baby."

Back up in the kitchen, Matt lost Colin and found himself standing in the kitchen. Dina had popped in, kissed him on the cheek, asked how he was doing, then floated away. A few women bustled around the island, preparing salads and humus. A blonde-headed pale woman brushed by him, holding a plate of shrimp and dip. Her face was garish with heavy makeup. "Try this," she said.

But he turned her down. "Not my thing."

"How do you not like shrimp?"

"Never did."

"Dina needs to hear about this," she said, flashing a big wacky smile before drifting away with her shrimp.

Another woman appeared, leaned into him and whispered, "I cannot stand that fucking idiot."

Matt was briefly stunned, but then he smirked. It was so random, so dry, so something his ex-wife, Megan, would say. Megan was always muttering under her breath. She'd been one of his co-workers, way back in the nineties. "Fucking moron," she'd hiss after her boss gave her something ridiculous to do. She'd been a part-time secretary, data-entry clerk while going to nursing school. It took about a year of joking together on the job, eating lunch, and then hanging out for drinks on Friday nights before Megan finally said, "So you gonna ask me out, lover boy?"

He sipped his beer. "Where you wanna go?"

Buying her diamond ring had been one of the scariest and happiest moments of his life. He'd gone into the diamond district in New York all by himself because that's what the guys on the job told him to do. "This ring is for life," the Hasidic man told him. It'd been a good marriage for a long time, until it wasn't. They had one son, Jake, who was in his freshman year at Stockton University in south Jersey. Matt refused to send him out of state claiming it was too expensive, but that wasn't the real truth. And he'd warned Jake not to pledge a fraternity.

"Takes up too much time and the guys are usually assholes. They do stupid shit." Matt had shifted nervously in his seat. Jake was driving.

"What stupid shit?" Jake said, glancing at his father.

Matt told him to keep his eyes on the road. "Just dumb, waste of time stuff. Get me a beer, do my chem homework. I don't know. Nothing good."

Nothing good. Never anything good.

"Caroline, the one who asked you if you wanted her shrimp,"

the whispering woman said, "yeah, she made the pesto over there. Last year someone found a fingernail in it."

Matt shook his head, a grin curling up his mouth.

She winked. "True story, darling," and drifted away.

He snuck outside after Dina had checked on him and then wandered away safely across the living room holding her glass of white wine, chatting with the fingernail woman, Caroline. Outside, the night seemed colder and sleet began to fall. Just as he was lighting up a bundled up family was making their way up the stairs. The woman was holding a shopping bag and two kids followed behind her. A man, wearing a knit dark-colored hat, was coming up the rear. Matt put his smoke in his mouth and held out his hand to help the woman as she just about reached the deck.

"Thank you," she said and in the white porch light, her eyes, round and wide, flicked to him for a beat, then flicked away.

The kids came up after, both in heavy puffy jackets, the daughter heavy-set and the boy short, about ten years old. The father, the man with the knit hat, stomped his feet at the top and huffed. "I'm out of shape," he said, and there, right there, when he lifted his head, when his voice was out in the air, it rushed back at Matt like a monster. The locked room. The stupid clown mask with the fuzzy red hair. Matt went into a shock, a moment of *What the Fuck? What the fuck!?* His heart thrashing and thrashing and thrashing.

"Dwight," the man said, holding out his gloved hand.

The cigarette was stuck between Matt's bare fingers, and he felt his throat close up, his heart still slamming, but like clockwork, instinct, something the body does to keep it safe, Matt switched his cigarette to his left hand and shook the man's gloved palm. It was as strong as he remembered it.

But Dwight didn't seem remember Matt. He just turned and followed his family inside.

***

"Fuck," Matt hissed to himself. Still standing, shaking. His eyes were watering. His teeth were chattering, his bones rattling. The cigarette was burning down to his skin and it hurt, but it took a long moment before he reacted, threw the butt away and stuck his hand on the deck railing where slushy ice had been gathering from the sleet. He lit another cigarette. His heart was still going. His brain unloading. Unloading the incident. The story. The story. *Fuck. Stop. Please stop.* Eighteen. He had been eighteen.

The ice continued to fall, and he strained to hear its quiet rapping as it fell on the trees up the hill but the muffled party drowned the sound out. He could hear Wendy cheering again, and Dwight shouting out to Colin. Matt smoked, wanting to tell someone. This is him! This is the motherfucker. For so long it felt like a dream, like something he watched in a movie, so unreal, so unreal he never quite believed it had happened. Even when he did admit it to Megan. Could he call Megan right now? Tell her? His former wife? She was the only one he could tell.

"He must've done it to other guys," she'd said once. "You should find them."

"How the fuck would I do that? 'Hey, you get locked in a room with this shitfuck Kappa Sig?'"

"You could meet up with men who went through something the similar. The guys who survived the Catholic church's scandal," she'd said. "They could help you. They'd understand."

Matt told her to get the fuck out of his face.

He went inside and heard Dwight right away, hooting. "Yeah, baby!" Dwight was like that. Hooting, yelling, calling out in that loud, heavy North Jersey/Staten Island accent. That old accent was fading, though. Matt heard it less and less these days.

"Gentrification," Megan had explained.

Matt didn't know what Dwight was hooting about. He only knew his blood felt thick, slow moving, but very red. He pictured the inside of his body like one of those *Blob* movies, maybe the 1972 version. The one where the kitten got stuck in the Blob's red gook as it slid across the floor.

He made his way over to the cooler and pulled out another beer. Stood by the wall again.

His burned finger was bothering him so he kept it against the bottle. Soon Dina was standing with him, holding her wine, her hand running under his shirt, along his lower back. It was meant to turn him on but he only pictured his skin opening, his thick blood oozing out. He pictured Dina's hand getting stuck in his Blob blood, the gook slowly moving up her arm, her screaming. "What's wrong with you? What the fuck is wrong with you!"

Megan had screamed those lines to him. "What the fuck is wrong with you! I'm trying here! I'm trying to fix us!" She'd cried so many tears over the years. But his confession that night after they'd taken nine-year-old Jake to the Museum of Natural History had killed everything. Matt had been watching his son pointing and grinning at the T-Rex and for some reason it was this that sent Matt back to that night at his Virginia college, had sent Matt thinking it could happen to his own boy one day, and these thoughts had made his throat close and his breath shallow, he raced down all those stupid little stairs they have at old museums, out onto Central Park West, and he kept walking, the cool air settling him, but he kept walking until he came upon The Dakota, where John Lennon was shot, where they'd used the building for the inspiration of *Rosemary's Baby*. He'd stood looking up at the spires and then the ugly gargoyles along the wrought iron fencing, his heart settling down, thinking about the movie, thinking about something he'd read once. Gargoyles, with their demonic faces and bodies, were considered protectors, and some considered them angels.

Later that night, when they were home in their little house in

New Jersey, he'd gone outside to smoke and drink and Megan had come out to join him and he'd confessed the story of the room in the frat house.

"Oh, Jesus," Megan said, sniffing, then crying. "Jesus."

The next morning he'd woken up dripping with shame. As if he'd done it again, this time willingly. He could barely look at his wife. Barely breathe in his own house.

Dina sipped her wine. "You okay, baby?" Matt kept drinking. Men came over, Dwight came over. They talked about this and that but a tin sound pierced in Matt's ears.

"I went to Montclair, in Jersey," Dina said.

Dwight said the name of the Virginia college he and Matt had both attended. Only Matt hadn't graduated. He'd dropped out in April. He'd been failing at that point, no need to stay. "What the fuck, Matt?" his father said when he came to pick him up. "You know how much money you made me waste?" Things got worse after that. Arguments, the drinking, weed, he wrecked his mother's Taurus. He started staying with a friend in a winter rental down in Seaside. More drinking, weed, girls he wasn't into but screwed anyway to prove he wasn't a faggot. That was the word he called himself over and over. "I'm a fucking faggot. Fag. Fag." He punched walls. Called women cunts. Smoked more weed. Did coke. Hell, he even got his hands on some heroin and snorted that a few times.

"I didn't go to college," Matt said. "No interest." This wasn't true. He'd been an honor student in high school, skinny, nice, cool. He loved science fiction, Ray Bradbury. He went to the movies with his mom all the time. He played basketball outside in the driveway with his younger brother. But after the incident that they didn't know about, after Matt went down the bad road, his family did the tough love thing with him. "You can't visit or hang out or even stay unless you pull your shit together." It was a royal mess until he got that job where he met Megan. But his mom, dad, brother, they still kept their distance. Even to this day.

"That's cool," Dwight said, raising his bottle. "You don't

have to go to college anymore. I tell my son that." His face was pinkish, puffy, and his hands were swollen like his stomach. His hairline was receding. The irony of life—the good-looking dudes get ugly. The skinny, weak dudes like Matt get mean.

The drinks were flowing and at times the kids came up from the lower level to grab food, pester their parents about going home, complain about being hit by some other kid, only to be shooed downstairs again.

Matt went outside but he found that he wasn't alone.

"Big smoker?" Colin asked, taking a cigarette from Matt.

"Sometimes."

The sleet had stopped, replaced by a cold rain.

Dwight stepped outside. Followed by the woman who muttered things under her breath. They bummed a cigarette off another guy standing near Colin. Dwight and the woman were laughing about Caroline, the woman with the shrimp. They were being cruel, laughing at her wide mouth and what she could fit in it. Megan had never been cruel like that.

Dwight made a joke and the woman who said things under her breath howled with laughter, rocked and fell back, slipped. Almost down the stairs. The edges of the small deck were icy. Colin grabbed her.

"Oh, fuck," she said.

Matt chucked the cigarette over the deck and went inside. His blood had loosened. He could feel it moving a little.

"Baby, are you okay?" Dina was wrecked. Her tiny body couldn't handle all that wine.

"Bathroom," he said, pulling away from her.

Safely concealed behind a locked door, he splashed water on his face. He took out his cell and pulled up Megan's number. They weren't divorced yet. After several years of her trying to get him to marriage counseling or any counseling, she'd given up. "I'm done." Separated and working through the paperwork, they had a mediator to keep things cheap. But he kept cancelling their sessions and rescheduling them. Work meeting. Dentist. All that stuff.

"Mom's seeing someone," Jake had confessed last week when Matt had driven down and taken him out to dinner. "Not a bad dude."

"Oh yeah?" Matt had said.

Jake glared at him for a long moment and then picked up his cheeseburger, shaking his head. "And he feels nothing."

In the light of the bathroom mirror, Matt was feeling something. He unlocked the door and went down into the basement. The kids were watching a movie. *Shrek.* Dwight's son was sitting on the floor with some Legos but his head was glued to the large screen. Jake had loved *Shrek.* He went around for months singing "All Star" by Smash Mouth. He still went around singing "All Star."

Do guys like Dwight do things to their own kids? Would that little boy sitting with his Legos, happily watching the green ogre have to...Matt told himself to stop. His blood was churning now, moving, rushing, bubbling to his brain. He was feeling that feeling again, that feeling he'd gotten in the museum, the feeling he got every so often, when he thought he might drop.

No, it was howl. He was feeling a beast might burst from his chest. An alien.

"You missed some great shrimp," Caroline said when he went upstairs. He was feeling bad for her for some reason. Her eye makeup was smudged and her face was glistening because the house was overheated. The woman who said things under her breath was flirting with Dwight. And Dwight's wife was sitting on a couch, watching, glowering. This is always how it went with parties like this. The kids locked down in the basement, the adults getting drunk and hitting on other people. Everything getting out of control, destabilizing marriages.

"You're too intense," Megan used to say when they were younger, before he'd confessed what he'd confessed.

And later, after the confession. "I want to help you," she said. "But I'm not equipped to handle it. The fact that you haven't done something, gotten some help is making it worse. I've been reading up on this—"

"You've been reading up on this," he'd growled, his back to her, his hands gripped on the edge of the kitchen counter, the noise from her mouth stewing a maniacal fury in him.

"Please, baby," she'd begged.

Matt saw himself that day, facing the kitchen window, his hand gripping the counter. "Will you please just shut the fuck up!"

His heart broke now. He was only mean to her like this when she brought up the story.

Dina was passed out next to Dwight's wife.

Wendy handed Matt another beer. "Dina could never hang."

The story went like this: Matt, eighteen, March, standing at a party in a frat house. The frat he desperately wanted to join because he knew it would help his sex life. He hadn't popped his cherry yet, but no one knew. He'd tried with his prom date, Jamie Selzman, but she said she didn't want the memory of her prom night to be about sex. "I need time. I need to be in a relationship."

So off he went to college, trying again with some cute girl from North Carolina, but he'd only gotten to third base. Of course he told his roommates he hit it hard. At the frat house, there weren't any girls because this was a rush party, the time to impress the older guys into letting him into their fraternity. Matt wasn't a big guy, wasn't super good-looking. Lanky, baby face, a nose that was a little wide and brown eyes. Dwight had approached him, a clown mask with the red frizzy hair sticking out on the sides, perched on top of his head. "Drink this, brother," he'd said, handing him a cup of red grain punch. "You should eat the fruit too." There were a couple pieces of melon floating in the cup. Then he nudged Matt in the side. "We've got some girls coming later. You like girls?"

Matt was nervous but he nodded. "Yeah. Oh yeah."

Dwight raised his eyebrows, smirked, nodded. "We'll get you set up tonight."

The girls did arrive and at that point, Matt was buzzing from the booze. Dwight introduced him to some of them, and they were nice, laughed at his jokes.

"Which one you like?" Dwight whispered.

Matt picked the pretty blonde wearing a short purple dress and choker necklace.

The plan was set—Matt was to go upstairs to the third floor, to the last room on the right and Dwight would send her up. "There's a small fridge in there. There's beer. Give her one."

"She's just gonna come up?" Matt said, feeling like he might be getting tricked or something, but Dwight seemed sincere.

"She'll be up," he said, patting him on the back.

Matt wandered up the first set of stairs, then another, then down the quiet, narrow hallway. He found the door and stood in the room, the muffled noise of the party pulsing underneath him. The walls were white, no posters, no clothes strewn around. Matt searched for the refrigerator but he couldn't find it. Soon the door opened. His heart battered. What would he say to her?

It wasn't he girl in the purple dress. It was Dwight, still wearing his clown mask. He locked the door behind him and pushed the mask over his face.

"Where's—" But Matt stopped talking. He knew. He'd heard the stories from his high school friends. Don't get drunk and pass out on the Boardwalk. Once this college guy got raped by a biker.

Matt tried to go for the door but Dwight grabbed him, rushed him to the bed, Matt's face on the pillow, the weight and force too strong to fight off, Dwight's hand on his head pushing it down. Dwight's hand jerking Matt's jean's down, Dwight's hand undoing his own pants, Dwight doing what he'd always set out to do. His breath hot on the back of Matt's neck. His grunts in his ear. The bed creaked loudly, a rhythmic sound, over and over and over again. The pain was so horrific, beastly, rotten, burning, devastating.

Afterwards, Dwight got up, fixed his pants and swiped the clown mask from the floor, where it had fallen after the initial struggle. He placed it over his face and left the room.

Matt, trying not to cry, got his pants on, got out into the hall, went down the stairs into the hot, loud, crowded party, and quickly slipped outside into the cool dark night. His ass hurt, and it would hurt for days. He told people he'd fallen on his butt after drinking too much grain. He never saw the girl in the purple dress again. He never thought she was in on it. She would go through life never knowing she had been used as bait.

Matt went outside to smoke again, the sleet still falling. He thought about standing in front of the Dakota. The gargoyles. The angels.

The door opened. Dwight, his big ugly body, stumbled onto the deck.

"You got one for me?" That old North Jersey/Staten Island accent.

Matt glared at him, the gargoyles in his wretched mind floating back to their corners.

"Sure." He pulled out a cigarette and handed it to Dwight. "Light?"

Matt stepped closer and lit Dwight's cigarette. Dwight sucked in the smoke hard, his big puffy hands holding the cigarette. He stared out, drunk. Matt looked at him, his heart pounding in quick, relentless beats. He felt the ruthless howl from his younger self. That horrific pain, humiliation, sadness, all of it bellowing from the deep hiding place in his chest, his soul. Dwight still didn't remember a thing, did he?

Had all of it not happened, Dwight and his stupid clown mask, had the girl in the purple dress come up instead, he would've stayed in college, gotten a different job, never met Megan and had Jake. The universe was cruel but when it was cruel, it changed the trajectory and sent you good things, but it didn't give you the resources to see it fully. It only gave you glimpses of the happiness you'd found.

"You still lock guys in rooms and jump on them?" Matt said.

Dwight's gaze shot from space to Matt.

"Your wife know?" Matt said.

Dwight blinked.

Matt moved to the edge of the small deck, near the stairs. The slippery, sleet covered-stairs. "You gonna do that to your boy?"

Just then the woman who whispered things, followed by Caroline who was all bundled up, appearing as if she were leaving, stepped outside. The woman who whispered things said, "I love being a bad kid," and Caroline said, "Smoking kills, you know," and Matt stared at Dwight who was staring back. It was coming to him.

"Bad kids," Matt said and there, right then, in a *What the fuck?* moment, Dwight snapped. He charged, but it was bumbled by his drunkenness, falling into Matt, who lifted up his arms, but knowing the two women were there, feigned a quick moment of help, pretending to go to grab him. Yet he didn't do a damn thing.

He let Dwight slip in the sleet and watched his puffy, gross body tumble and roll and slide and fall to the bottom. The women screamed but Matt didn't.

At the bottom of the stairs, Dwight's body lay motionless on the driveway, the sleet falling down.

***

The kids cried, the people at the party cried, the police came, the EMTs arrived, but Dwight's neck was broken. He was dead.

"Usually drunk people survive things like that," Matt overhead a cop say, then chuckle.

They asked Matt questions but it was Caroline who told the story. "Dwight was so drunk. He just tripped into Matt and Matt tried to grab him but he had a cigarette in his hand. Had he not had that cigarette..." She turned her head to Matt and for a moment he thought it might spin all the way around.

It was ruled an accident.

The next day Matt left Dina in Connecticut. She wanted to stay with Wendy and Colin, and she wanted him to stay with her.

"Not doing that," he said.

He drove away, away from New England, over the Táppan Zee Bridge, the heavy overcast clouds hovering over the Hudson River. Guilt snaked through him. Shame oozed through his veins. He'd done a bad thing. But his head was clearing. *This is what real revenge feels like.*

He saw his younger self crying in his quiet dorm room.

When he reached New Jersey, the sun came out.

THE HAPPIEST MEAL

James R. Tuck

I'm coming around the dumpster, struggling up the hill in these big floppy fucking shoes, when I hear a laugh.

I turn and look and there's this kid leaning on the side of the dumpster. He's got shaggy hair hanging out from under his uniform cap, and a big, fat joint to his lips.

The floppy fucking shoes make little *slap slap* noises on the asphalt as I walk over to him.

"Something funny, motherfucker?"

He giggles again, and snorts with the smoke, "Now, that right there is some funny shit."

Sweat breaks free from my hairline and runs quick over the greasepaint and down onto my neck as I stand there deciding what to do with this little prick. I oughta show him what I've got. That'll shut him up.

He holds out the joint. "Want to hit this?"

And all of a sudden, ain't nothing more in the world I want to do than to Hit. That. Joint.

I *slap slap* closer to him and squeeze in the shade by the dumpster. Damn, food garbage smells worse than anything on a ballsack-hot summer day in Georgia.

"You here for the birthday parties?"

"There's more than one birthday party?"

73

"Ha ha, yeah, which one are you here for?"

"Is one of them more annoying than the other?"

"One of them, the kids are okay, kind of loud but not too bad. They don't want anything extra and I haven't made too big a mess for me to clean up. The other one's a church group, Brown-Eye Baptist Church or some shit. Those little motherfuckers are just wrecking the playground."

He holds up the joint.

"That's why I'm out here getting my head right."

I take the joint from him, pulling a big old drag of the sticky sweet deep in my lungs. The kid's shit is dank but it does the job.

I think about all those kids. Sure, their meals are only three or four bucks, but that shit adds up. The registers are probably full by now.

Could be a decent score.

That's not why I'm here, not today, but I file the idea in the back of my mind for another time.

I hand him back the joint. It's stained red from the greasepaint around my mouth.

"'Preciate it. I guess I better get to work."

"Yeah, man," he says. "I'll head in with you."

I shake my head, the cotton candy hair that juts out to the sides sways as I do and I have to adjust the tiny hat on top of my bald cap. "Naw, you should stay and finish that, I'm about to get those little fuckers all worked up, so you're going to need the extra chill."

He takes another drag and squints at me. "You right, you right," he says, sliding down to sit on the ground.

I leave him there, slap slapping my way across the drive-through. I hope my parole officer doesn't pop me with a piss test next week, 'cause he ain't going to like that THC in my system.

I put the thought out of my mind as I open the door and the air conditioning hits my face. It smells like French fries and I can feel the greasepaint on my face tightening up from it.

People look up as I *slap slap* through but I ignore them motherfuckers. I'm here for Charlie.

People stop looking when I get to the door for the indoor playground. I stand there with my hands on the bar handle looking for him but I don't see him. He's probably at the top of the climbing thing.

He's going to be so surprised.

"Excuse me."

I turn and there's a lady standing there with a tray full of food and two tow-headed little brats next to her.

"Excuse me, we need to get by."

She's not bad looking, a little frumpy, her Homecoming Queen days long behind her. Speaking of behinds, the two brats and a tray full of food haven't done it any favors.

I push the door open and hold it for them as they come in.

She doesn't say thank you.

Why is it so loud in here?

Like every kid is screaming at the top of their lungs like little savages.

And it's hot.

Like all the breath these kids are exhaling is just stuck in this room, hanging in the air like a smog of hot CO2 and French fry grease-tainted moisture.

My jumpsuit is swampy in the crotch.

I keep looking up in the apparatus, trying to spot Charlie. He's the only one of these little bastards I care about.

I haven't seen him in forever.

"You're late."

I turn and there she is.

She looks good. She's changed her hair color, from her normal chestnut brown to a dark red with some purple highlights, and she cut it short. It frames her face, drawing the eye to her mouth, which is always her best and worst feature. I don't get to look down and see if she's lost any weight before she starts in.

"Did he tell you the wrong time? I bet he fucked that up."

"Beverly," I say. "Chill the fuck out. I'm here, ain't I?

Her squinty eyes squint harder as she looks at me closely then widen as she realizes it's me.

"Chet? What are you doing?"

"You said I could get him a clown for his birthday."

"Yeah, you could get him a clown. You can't show up here dressed as a clown."

"I just wanted to see him."

I didn't say: And clowns are fucking expensive.

"You can't see him, idiot. There's a restraining order for a reason."

"Come on, Bev. I did my time for that."

"You'll never do enough time for that. You hurt him."

"I turned my back for one fucking second. I didn't know he was going to touch the damn saw. He should have stayed—"

"Don't!"

She's up in my face, finger pointing, so close her nail scratches the greasepaint on my cheek. "Don't you dare blame him. You were fucked up when you should have been paying attention."

She takes a deep whiff, putting her nose right up against my chest.

"Are you high right now?"

Shit.

"No, that's just—"

"I can't fucking believe you. You show up here, violate the order, you're high, and—" she steps back and looks me up and down. "What is this outfit you're wearing?"

"I'm a clown. Ain't that obvious?"

"Yeah, but I've seen this clown before."

"You don't know this clown, don't worry about it."

She studies me with her face pinched tight. It makes me want to fiddle with the outfit, adjust the frilled collar around my neck, push the little hat upright on my head, but I hold still.

She don't know this clown. She never cared about this shit.

Never cared about anything I like.

She don't know this clown.

Her eyes open wide with surprise, then cloud with anger.

"I know this fucking clown."

Shit.

"You come here to your son's birthday party dressed like a serial killer clown?"

"Beverly, calm the fuck down, he don't know who John Wayne Gacy is."

Her mouth turns mean, snake mean. "And you wonder why I don't want him around your fucked-up ass? It's shit just like this."

"Shit just like what? Shit just like a dad trying to see his fucking son on his birthday? Shit like trying to make him laugh by dressing like a fucking clown?"

"If you don't see how fucked up it is that you come to your child's birthday party dressed the same way a serial killer used to dress so he could kill kids then I can't even talk to you."

"Lots of people like serial killers, Bev. It doesn't make me a bad guy."

She laughs, harsh and sharp like a slap. "Oh you wish you were a bad guy but you're not, Chet, you're just a fuck up. Charlie's the only reason I don't regret fucking you."

I lean forward, close to her face. "Well, I'm here now and I'm going to see him."

She shoves me.

It takes me by surprise and I stumble back. These big floppy fucking shoes get caught in the wide legs of the striped jumpsuit I'm wearing and I lose my balance. I don't get my hands out in front of me in time and I catch myself on my face.

The tile floor is hard.

Harder than my tooth. It snaps right off at the gum and starts rattling around in my mouth. The pain of it is hot lightning that shoots up to the corner of my eye.

And even as my eye starts watering I realize the entire place has gone dead silent.

I roll over and everybody is looking at me.

All the parents.

All the kids.

Beverly.

Charlie.

He's at the top of one of the slides, and his little eyes burn right through me, staring with an intensity that's not supposed to be in the face of a child.

And then some motherfucker laughs.

A big dude in a flannel shirt who's standing at the end of the table beside Beverly's mom. He's got a big laugh from his big gut and it rolls up into the wide-open indoor playground echoing off all that plastic and Plexiglas.

And then all the motherfuckers start laughing.

I try to get up as my mouth fills with blood but the big floppy fucking shoes keep me from getting my feet under me and my legs get all tangled up in the jumpsuit.

The hat falls off my head and rolls across the tile.

The white cotton gloves on my hands keep sliding on the tile.

By the time I come up to my feet I've lost one of the shoes, blood is dripping down my chin and onto my big frilly collar, and my hair has come loose from the shitty rubber band that was holding it under the bald cap and now it lays on my face sticking to the greasepaint.

And all the motherfuckers are roaring.

Please don't let him…

I look up and Charlie is laughing too.

My stomach falls into an endless black void that has opened up inside my body and I don't feel anything, just a cold numbness that seems to try to pull me down.

Beverly's laughing so hard her face has turned purple and tears are streaming down her cheeks.

This is all her fault. I had a good life before she kicked me out. Maybe I didn't have a job but I had a family and things were starting to happen for me. But oh no, one little accident and all of a sudden I'm "not safe" to be around my son and I can't live in my house and I can't fuck my wife.

She wouldn't even bring him to visit me in prison.

"I'm his fucking dad!" I scream at her.

The laughs stop like someone yanked the plug on a sound system.

The silence breaks into people yelling at me, calling me names and saying terrible, threatening things about me.

They all shut the fuck up when I pull the gun out from under my coveralls.

I point it all of them, swinging it from one side of the room to the other, staring at their dumb, blank looks.

"Not so funny now is it, motherfuckers?"

"Chet," Beverly says. "What are you doing?"

I lunge at her, shoving the gun in her face. "You should have brought him to visit me."

She stumbles back and falls on her ass. The big guy and the flannel shirt starts moving our way.

I see the determination on his face and realize he's probably fucking her.

I swing the gun his direction. "Stop right there, you shitfuck redneck, or I'll blow your goddamn brains out."

He skids to a stop and puts his hands up.

"Now, there's no call for—"

I move over toward him, only one floppy fucking shoe slapping on the tile. "Don't you tell me what there's no fucking call for. I didn't ask your opinion."

I can smell the fear coming off of him and it gets me higher than that hit off the joint outside did. His eye is twitching and I can see a little reflection of me holding the gun. He knows I could do it. I could pull this trigger and put him out of my misery.

He thinks I'm a hard man.

And he's right.

Right this minute, I am a hard man. I'm the baddest mother-fucker there is.

And then Beverly opens her goddamn mouth.

"Stop it! You're scaring him to death!"

For a minute I think she's talking about this redneck here in front of me.

And then I realize what she means.

I turn and she's kneeling with her arms around Charlie. He's crying from eyes as wide as saucers.

He looks just like he did that day that I wasn't paying attention to him.

That day he got hurt.

Because of me.

Because I'm a fuck up, not a hard man.

And just like that, every ounce of homicidal rage drains right out into my one floppy fucking shoe.

The gun seems to weigh forty pounds in my hand.

"Get out," I say.

Nobody moves.

I raise the gun in the air like I'm going to fire it.

"Everybody get the fuck out of here! Right now!"

That gets them moving.

They herd up and shove their way out like cattle in a stampede. It takes a few minutes for everybody to squeeze through the one door. I watch some little girl with pigtails get knocked down and start crying and the adult not even turn around.

By the time they all get outside of the room there's flashing blue lights chasing each other around the walls through the windows from outside.

They'll be here in a minute.

I shuffle over to the table, one floppy fucking shoe slapping on the tile, and have a seat.

The blood in my mouth from the broken tooth tastes like shit.

The tooth isn't in my mouth anymore. Huh, I swallowed that damn thing at some point. I reach over, pick up a cup, and take a drink through the straw.

Fucking Sprite.

I hate Sprite.

There's a half-eaten cheeseburger laying on a wrapper and even though it's cold I take a big bite of it so that the last thing I taste isn't going to be fucking Sprite and blood.

I'm still chewing when they come through the door, AR-15s raised to their shoulders. They are head-to-toe in black fatigues, pads on their elbows and knees, shit hanging off their belts like some kind of superheros, and helmets with Plexiglass shields.

Damn, S.W.A.T. looks impressive.

They're yelling at me to drop my weapon and get down on my belly.

They don't know that I didn't have any money for bullets.

And it doesn't matter.

I swallow the mouthful of shitty cheeseburger and point my empty gun at the police.

Happy birthday, Charlie.

TAKING FLESH
Chuck Regan

*The word Carnival originates from
the Latin carne vale, "Flesh, farewell."*
—The Facts on File Encyclopedia
of Word and Phrase Origins, 3rd Ed.

Dan's older brother Bobby slurped around a mouth full of Cheerios when he told us the carnival had set up in the middle of the night.

We thought he was just fucking with us. He fucked with us a lot, particularly me. Bobby said he thought at first it was cops with all the lights and how late it was. Someone was always calling the cops on Bobby and his friends. He said he stuck around and watched the carnies unload and get drunk. He said they had some real freaks working this year.

This was in August, 1983. I was fourteen years old that summer and a growth spurt had left me gawky and pimpled and easily six inches taller than the bullies who used to pick on me.

Dan—my best friend since first grade—had been trying on a tough-guy persona, mirroring his big brother. In the next month, he and I would be freshmen in high school, a big change.

I was scared to death, but I couldn't admit that to Dan.

Bobby, the soon-to-be-senior, told us stories about how the seniors locked freshmen onto the roof, stole their clothes out of the locker room, and burned them with cigarettes and beat up anyone they didn't like.

Bobby had taken every opportunity to terrify us with the details of what we should expect from high school. I didn't have an older brother to tell me what it was really going to be like, and the more scared I got, the more short-tempered Dan had become with me. I was surprised when Dan said he wanted to go to the carnival with me. It seemed like such a little kid thing to do.

"It's a different crew," Dan's big brother said before going back to his room. "…after what happened to those kids last year."

We had all heard the stories. Three kids got killed last year.

We got on our bikes to go check it out.

As soon as we rode over the top of the hill, a bright red Ferris wheel broke the familiar tree line of the woods. We sped down to get close.

All the machines were quiet. Wooden wedges were jammed against the tires. Painted-on grinning clowns and snarling animals glowered at us—their faces chipped and streaked with oil and rust. A chain clanked against an aluminum pole in a steady rhythm, stirred by a cool breeze blowing across the neighboring soccer field, carrying the smell of diesel and stale cigarettes. Nobody was around.

"Bobby had sex for the first time at a carnival," Dan said, dropping his kickstand.

Not knowing how to respond to this information, I just said, "Really?"

"Yeah. Behind the funhouse. He was thirteen, and she was a junior in high school," Dan said with pride.

We walked past the empty ticket booth, and my bowels gurgled. We circled the parking lot, looking at all the machines until there was nothing more to see. I turned to ask Dan if he was ready to leave, but he had walked off. I got a creepy feeling like he had been kidnaped by the carnies, but I found him standing, looking up at one ride.

"It was this one," Dan said.

The Salt and Pepper Shaker—two long, blue arms with licks of fire painted down the sides. Two caged baskets were ready to grab handfuls of screaming children and toss them into the sky.

"A bolt came loose and the cage flew off. It crashed over there."

Dan pointed to a pile of old splintered bleachers overgrown with weeds.

"They put those there to cover up the blood stains."

Bobby had put a bug up Dan's ass that it was his turn to get laid, like he'd be disowned if he didn't get this rite of passage out of the way before he entered high school. But Dan was doughy and weak-chinned, and I was scrawny and pimply and socially inept. Neither of us had had any luck with girls so far, so I knew we needed a plan if we were going to have any kind of shot at finding any young women willing to deflower us.

The previous year, I had taken a summer class in photography and knew enough about my father's vintage Rangefinder 35mm camera to load the film and focus it. The plan was to pretend to be working for the school newspaper and lure in some girls by appearing important. That night, I dressed in what I thought were my coolest clothes, slung the camera around my shoulder like it was a rifle, and rode my ten-speed to the high school.

Dan met me at the far end of the soccer field. His hair was slicked back, and he was wearing his brother's old leather jacket. He looked ridiculous, but I looked even more awkward standing next to him in my outdated jeans and a Van Halen T-shirt I had never worn before.

"Let's do this," sounding like he was leading the A-Team as he pulled a plastic wrapper out of his pocket. It looked like an oversized Lifesaver candy. I nodded, but it was the first time I had ever seen a condom. Dan nodded to me, like he was definitely going to get some use out of it, but his self-assurance was lost on me. I just nodded back.

The carnival was already filled. I saw girls from my classes and some out-of-town girls that looked dangerous. I rated each of them in my head, but was too nervous to raise the camera to them. Dan tried to get me warmed up, pointing out scenes for me to photograph. Every time he raised his hands to frame his fingers into L's, the leather sleeves of his jacket creaked like an old chair. It was a cool night for August but he was sweating, and I was laughing. He told me to shut up and be serious.

He pulled me to the cotton candy vendor, where three girls in bright pink shorts were standing, eating mounds of spun blue sugar.

"Hey, girls, how about a shot for the paper?" he said. Slick.

They sneered, called us little pervs, and walked away, sneering. Dan's face got red as he watched them go. His nose dripped sweat.

"This is bullshit." Dan said, taking off the jacket.

"Let's do the bumper cars," I said.

"Fuck off. Leave me alone," he said.

I stood in the middle of the squall of lights and colors and cotton candy and sweat and watched him walk away. I should have been angry, I guess. For as long as I've known him, he had never talked to me like that.

Just as I was about to run after him, a man started hollering in a loud, angry voice. I heard a slap and a grunt and then a girl shrieked Stop! Two grown men were fighting over a stuffed Garfield doll at the water gun booth. Snarls of rage pinched at their lips, glaring their cold eyes at each other, fists flying and hands grabbing shirts. I raised my camera.

Click.

Kids and adults pushed past me to get a clearer view of the fight. Two women with cut-off sweatshirts nudged into view. Their faces peeled into feral glee as blood bloomed at the corner of the one man's mouth. I advanced the film and took aim at the girls' expressions.

Click.

The stink of body odor and funnel cake washed past me as two cops raced in to break it up.

Click.

The crowd booed and threw bits of caramel corn at the cops as they pulled the two men away. As the crowd parted, a carny—gaps in his teeth, bags under his eyes, hint of a skull tattoo under his shirt sleeve—grinned at the drama.

Then, he smiled at me like I was the only one there. The strobing lights made the shadows on his face dance. I raised my camera to him.

Click.

Like some psychotropic gas was pumping out of the machines, I felt a hunger—not for food, but for something much deeper—I wanted more fights. I wanted to capture every sweat-clinging skirt and grimace at the patrons.

Something took me over then.

I rode the rides just to frame faces rippling with terror and elation as they flew through the night, strapped into deathtraps. I was caught up in a storm of flashing lights, the stink of fried food, and fear. I was just a ghost. Nobody seemed to notice me.

When I advanced the film and felt the tug at the end of the roll, a chill ran up my back.

I had only brought one roll with me, and now it was over. I had been expelled from heaven.

During my sophomore year at college, I interned with Gerald Eiger—a wedding photographer. He seemed at first apologetic for exposing me to his world of complimentary drinks and Vaseline-smeared lenses. I guess he could sense that I thought I was better than him. I was just an asshole kid with a scholarship and a decent eye for composition. After I got the stick of pretension out of my ass, I learned a lot from him.

Gerry was a master at working with available light to frame a shot or to chisel a subject out of shadow. He instinctively knew the best locations for the obligatory shots—the cake, the dress, the ringed fingers—and how to work the aperture to turn the ugliest wallpaper or cheap plastic shrubs into mysterious, ethereal backgrounds.

On my first wedding shoot at a VFA, he assigned me the candid shots. I stood back from the smiling crowds and aimed at the people I thought were most likely to crack their facade of civility. The theme I gave myself was to expose the secret meanings of the rituals of marriage. I wanted to capture the worried looks of the soon-to-be mothers-in-law, the proud and jealous glances of the bridesmaids. Later, at the reception, I photographed the sixty-year-old aunts dirty dancing and leering like they were eighteen, and the teenaged nephews drunk off of abandoned champagne.

Back at his studio, after my rolls were developed, Gerry told me to stop thinking like an anthropologist and more like a game show host. He insisted that our job was to capture the illusion of marriage, not the reality. The clients wanted to see what they thought love was supposed to look like—misty roses and eternal smiles. He told me that they would discover the truth on their own soon enough. Let them have their illusions while they could.

I kept doing what I wanted to do. He smiled, shook his head and told me that I was just wasting film. People don't want to see themselves. They want to see what they hope to see.

"But I want to wake them up!" I said.

"Let 'em sleep."

* * *

After I earned my BFA, I got a job at a local newspaper—photographing high school sports, teen pageants, and events at the mall. I kept telling myself that if I traveled to different assignments, I would eventually discover subject matter worthy of a project—a thesis to focus on, a truth to reveal.

I submitted what I thought was my best work to regional photography competitions. I received just enough recognition to compel my ego to keep going. I convinced myself I was going to hit the big time eventually. My overenthusiastic ego wrote off my lack of success on the stupidity of the judges. They just didn't understand what I was trying to say.

After two years of nothing to add to my portfolio, no awards to brag about, and no decent meals to put on my table, I had to start doing weddings.

Gerry was right—my analytical candids were always rejected by clients. They only wanted the faerie tale shots. I threw my best candids into a shoebox and gave notice at the paper. I committed myself to being mediocre with a fully stocked fridge.

Weddings required more labor than I had anticipated. Between assembling the books and promoting the business, I found myself reciting Gerry's same placating mantra: At least I'm working in my field, as I sat holding a glue gun and glitter at a night school scrapbooking class.

I had plodded my way into hell, and whimsical stickers and corn husk raffia were the only coins I had to offer to the ferryman.

My last assignment with the paper was to photograph a sculptress in her studio. Her only claim to fame was that a large piece of hers had been installed in the courtyard of a newly constructed corporate center. The blocky, oppressive buildings were expected to enliven a small suburban town's economy, and anyone involved in the project was deemed newsworthy by the paper's editors.

I drove to the site and photographed the sculpture. The iron rebar-and-bronze thing was vaguely orb-shaped, with chrome tubes weaving in and out of its surface like a time-lapse photo of air traffic taking off and landing on a ruined Earth. I didn't understand what it was supposed to represent, and I judged the hell out of the artist as being a talentless hack who just fumbled out any nonsense her hands fumbled together.

The world was upside down when true artists were relegated to crap jobs, and hacks like this woman got big commissions to spew out soulless shit. Some idiot in a suit, his tie cutting off all circulation to his brain, decided that because he didn't understand the sculpture, it must have profound meaning. Soon enough, business-casual drones would be eating lunch under this thing's shadow, while my career continued to rot in obscurity.

I used a little of Gerry's techniques to bring out the textures, but the buildings were important to the context of the story, so I framed a few compositions—click, click, click—documentation.

I arrived late to the sculptress's studio. The reporter writing the story had already left, and the artist was eager to continue work on her latest project. I apologized for being late. Her hands were covered in clay and she apologized for not shaking my hand. In the middle of the garage studio was an oversized Gumby-like fern-arch-thing she intended to cast in bronze—a commission for a bank. She seemed in a daze as she told me to photograph whatever I wanted. She didn't care. She was getting paid.

As I looked around her unimposing studio, she worked the clay, unenthusiastic, yet committed to the task—as if she were monotonously feeding a monstrous toddler gaping with bottomless hunger. My jealously for her success began to shift. I could see that she was trapped in her role.

Her hands moved in a meditation, slow and deliberately applying globs of clay—the final shape of the thing was some kind of inevitability that would be revealed to her. She had no control over it. She was merely fulfilling the role of a factory worker assembling parts designed by some other entity—some demon buried deep inside her subconscious.

I learned something important in that studio.

The artist, whose name I forget, had found the means for perpetual expression—one project paying her living expenses until the next project. She was living every artist's dream, but she seemed bored—imprisoned, like Gerry, like me. Her attitude toward her craft fascinated me. She was no longer struggling to prove anything to herself, and the money kept coming in. Her patrons demanded she produce more of whatever it was she had to say. I wondered if she had anything left to say, or if she was dried up like the cutesy-crafty, sun-bleached scarecrow planted awkwardly in the overgrown garden outside the studio window.

I stayed for almost an hour snapping pictures. I didn't bother her with conversation, and she didn't seem affected by my presence at all. Her paint-spattered boombox, peppered with scorch marks, scraped out rambling late '70s prog rock as I lurked through her studio. Scribbled notes and crumpled sketches formed a nest woven with grocery lists and to-do lists—the exposed mind of a well-fed artist.

The sun dipped lower. The light crawled in through the big windows and onto her earth-clotted hands, burning there, providing a contrast on her smooth puckered flesh to a shadow on the sharp volcanic textures of the clay. Where does the artist end and the art begin?

The photos that came out of that session were the best I had taken since that night at the carnival when I was fourteen. I submitted the batch to a national arts magazine and they were enthusiastically accepted. The feature photo in my submission was the close up of her hands—her weedy, cinderblock garden providing Gerry-techniqued backlighting. To me, the shot perfectly expressed the melancholy of an artist's isolation.

There was no bigger thrill than seeing my work published.

When I received my comp copy of the arts magazine, I drank a bottle of pinot noir in celebration.

I dreamt of the carnival that night.

I've had the same dream for twenty years. I am fourteen years old, snapping photos of a carousel. Gold, cream, and blue antique horses waltz around a gaudy calliope as it brays vaudevillian dirges.

When I stop to load another roll of film, I drop my lens cap and it rolls under the ride. I duck down under the guard rail to retrieve the cap but I am pulled back by rough hands. The skull-tattoo carny from the photo breathes a rotted-teeth-and-cigarette breath onto my face and says, "You don't belong here." His words resonate nasally with a marshmallow hollowness. In recent replays of the dream, I have come to suspect that he has a cleft palate.

His calloused palm scratches my arm as he pulls me toward the house of mirrors then pushes me in. Actually, no. Every time I've had the dream, I just appear inside. There is no door I pass through. I've had the dream so many times, I usually realize at this point that I am dreaming and walk through the rest of it, waiting for it to end.

This particular night I had the dream, I wondered if the mirrors were supposed to represent all the photographs I've taken—distorted representations of myself.

I shuffle my way around the mirrors, kicking aside paper cups, avoiding the cotton candy cones stuck to the dusty plywood floorboards, and the weather-beaten painted Victorian poster of a clown dressed in a tutu. The deeper I go, the thicker the dust gets until it becomes the dirt floor of a natural cave. Broken pottery and bones are half buried in the slate-stinking dust.

The passage narrows and I have to crawl. I scrape my elbows and knuckles and wonder if I will wake up with scabs. The cave opens up to a cold, empty darkness. Primitive drawings are sketched on the walls in black and rust red. I try to study the drawings—I know they are important. It is always at this point that I wake up.

There are parts of the dream that change.

Sometimes, I find a door to my parents' basement, and once or twice there was a washing machine or a set of industrial shelves with my old toys on it.

The carny's face is always the same. I can never remember the specifics of what is drawn on the cave walls, but every morning after I have that dream, I feel the urge to find a carnival. I fantasize that some state fair somewhere nearby has the door I need to find into this House of Mirrors.

With a pinot noir hangover the morning after the dream, I had just sit down to do a search for a local carnival when Todd my booking agent called me with a last-minute gig. A seventy-fifth wedding anniversary party. I refused the job. I lied and told him I had a conflict. I had no plans, but I had to do something else. If it wouldn't be a carousel, I would photograph an old bridge, or an automotive graveyard. I needed to find something, anything other than photographing the lies of smiling people.

In suburban Eastern Pennsylvania, carnivals exist, but they are too bright, too clean, too sterile. Neutered. Maybe it was because the rides were set up on the campuses of a Christian school or on church grounds, or the rides are too freshly painted. Maybe the kids are too happy, or not scared enough.

Something was radically different in those carnivals from that one I remembered. There was no danger present—no seething sexuality. Even after the sun had set, these carnivals never transformed beyond bland, clip-art caricatures. I deleted all but a few mediocre pictures on my digital camera. Wasted trips, I dismissed four wedding gigs, and overdrew my bank account twice.

I fought off the toxic shininess of the winter holidays as if it were cancer, taking regular chemo treatments of scotch and bourbon. I sneered at the sight of each Nativity, each rosy-cheeked Santa, and every candy-light-decorated porch even while I photographed them. I still had to make a living. I submitted these photos to stock photography websites, and royalty checks fell randomly into my Stripe account like coins from the sky.

Hunting these kitchy pics, I always made sure nobody was home. I carry model release forms with me in case I get confronted and have to ask permission to use the photos, but negotiating licensing is a pain in the ass, and a waste of time, and a potential bleed on what little money I make. This one time, someone was home, but I couldn't resist. I climbed onto their front porch and used Gerry's lighting techniques, pulling my focus onto interesting details of lights and snow-dusted fir tree fronds. I clicked off a few shots that would make good schmaltzy greeting card covers, but every chirp of my digital camera only confirmed that I was no longer able to travel inside of that little heaven of the framing window where I had been safely transported that first night at the carnival.

Of course, I had tried many times to expand my technique. An artist's expression is influenced by many things, including the tools he uses. I had switched to a digital medium almost a decade ago, but I occasionally experimented with old cameras—Polaroids and box cameras until the film was no longer produced. I used infrared film, warping lenses, filters, and digital filters—but each photo I took with those gimmicks felt painfully self-conscious, like something a student would produce hoping their new tools would do the work for them. No matter what I tried, I just confirmed I was a fraud.

When the owners opened their front door, I thanked them a little too enthusiastically for kicking me off their property. I was done pretending to be something I wasn't.

***

I resumed my search for carnivals at the first signs of spring. In late March, I found one in Maryland. I dug out my old Canon A-1 from the back of my closet and a box of Kodak Tri-X black-and-white film from the freezer—the film had a nice grain to it, and great contrast in low light. If I was a fraud, this film would confirm it—it told no lies, only enhanced what I was exposing it to. I threw some road snacks and a thermos of coffee into the car and took off.

I had driven through an hour of rain after an unseasonably hot afternoon, and when I pulled into the parking lot of the sleeping carnival, the dusky sun was struggling to burn its way through storm clouds, a thin mist writhing on the ground. The gates were wide open but rides were dark, the kiosks open for business. Nobody was inside them, like they had all been snatched away by some beast of local folklore. Full soggy trashcans reeked of spoiled meat and day-old vomit. The place had a dirty, hurried-taboo-sex feeling to it.

It was perfect.

The rain had cast everything in deep contrast. Shadowed surfaces were black mirrors that warped the world around them. The water drops clinging to every edge chimed with golden light.

Happy elephants were anchored to the legs of a bright red robot spider. Dead gray lights were planted in rows along its spiral limbs, like eyes of some primordial creature threatening to open. I switched to my macro lens and got in tight on one of the fiberglass elephants hastily airbrushed in grey and pink. A scar—a dead-fish-colored fibrous chunk was taken out of its trunk. Click. Pistons dripping oily fluid were framed in the shadow of a clown head. Click. The sign Jumbo Whirl was painted in cotton candy colors, encircled by light bulbs arranged in a dance of dead glass reflecting the milk-clouded sky. Click.

I stepped back and tried to remember how it felt to be a child, climbing aboard my first ride. These beasts were nothing like the buzzing ponies or shimmying helicopters stationed outside of grocery stores. As big as a small car, the fiberglass creatures would fling tiny bodies around in ways no child could be accustomed in their normal world, rising higher than any tree they had ever climbed, spinning in circles designed to disorient. I wondered how many children had been initiated by this particular ride, and how many had puked on the seats. Still, the elephants and clowns smiled, in spite of this. Click.

I moved on to the Ring of Fire, a five-story vertical black hoop painted with flames—an alien hot rod prepped for takeoff. Or maybe it was an astronomical marker erected by ancient aliens. Fractured by the tree line, the sun peeked through the ring, shining a sharp, golden crescent on its center rail.

Each click of the shutter pulled me in deeper. Tighter compositions. Deeper contrasts. Sharper focus on the grime-crusted details.

The mystic morphine that drives every artist and athlete was rushing through me. I hadn't had to hand-return a roll of film for years, and I actually felt fear—fear that I wouldn't be able to get back inside that framing window, into that zone, but when I advanced past the last frame and felt it pull taut at the end of the spool, I knew my hunger was back. It had been such a long time since I had been that deep inside of that tiny window, I had forgotten how time can distort. The sun was gone, and so was my contrast.

I grinned like a madman as I spun the tiny lever on the camera, listening to the plastic clatter as tiny teeth pulled the exposed film back into its black shell. A drunken nostalgic thrill welled up in me. When the roll spun freely inside the camera, I felt as though I had retrieved a dream. I took out the roll and patted it in my pocket as if it were an engagement ring, then loaded the next roll.

I had been so caught up in my bliss, before I finished the next roll, I was shocked to see people stepping into my line of sight. The carnies had opened their games and prepped the rides as I had been traveling through a parallel dimension. The mist was long gone, banished by the hard tinny speakers blaring forty year old rock music. Animated lights blinked anemically in the fading light. The rides began to spin, and as if lured in by their movement, people arrived.

Stuffed animals clutched in their grip, children swaggered through the crowds displaying the trophies they had killed with darts, ping-pong balls, or water pistols. Teens ranging from lanky twigs to fully-blossomed proto-adults crowded around the booths. Boys masked in painted-on machismo demonstrated their impending manhood to every female within range as they hunted plush prey.

And there it was.

A gawky boy, about fourteen years old, bent over to throw a ring onto a bottle—a fierce concentration burned in his eyes. Three girls his age stood in the background. The one farthest from him snuck a look past her friends at him. She licked an ice cream cone as her hair draped coquettishly over half her face.

Here were the ancient fertility rites. Here was a proving ground for hunters—an otherworldly spectacle of lights and sound designed to bring forth a shift in consciousness—one that has been part of the human condition since before the written word. Here was our modern Stonehenge—a garishly lit circle made out of aluminum and chipped paint.

Here, the sacrifices were not in blood, but of money and ego, but the rituals were the same.

Spinning in circles the participants couldn't control, fear and a distortion of reality assaulted them. The games of chance were a reinforcement of that distortion—a player knows he should be able to toss a ring onto a post, or knock over a small stack of cups with a baseball. These hunters are told that their reality is not as solid as they had imagined. The carnies were trickster-shamans, humbling those who were not aware that their world was not entirely solid.

* * *

I spent that spring and summer driving across the tri-state area. Each carnival pulled me further into understanding these old rituals. Each roll of film explored my thesis more deeply, Carnival as Ritual Space.

Click. An obese family—their sausage fingers gripping bags and cones stuffed with multicolored foods of spun sugar and fried meat. Clots stuck to their necks and faces and shirts, they are sacrificial beasts stuffed for the feast.

Click. A young woman on a tilt-a-whirl is clinging desperately to her boyfriend. Her hair is whipped into a frenzy and her eyes are closed as some otherworldly puppet master tugs at her body. A mix of ecstasy and fear curl around her mouth—an orgasmic smile.

Click. A carnie throws his head back as he bellows to announce the next game. A demonic gleam in his eye threatens the camera to not reveal his secrets.

For the next few months, I focused on finding an agent, approving the layout of a book, then publishing and promoting it. That next spring, the book's premiere sold less than three thousand copies nationwide. Angela, my agent, assured me that those numbers were good considering it was my first coffee table book—I hate that phrase—and especially good considering my subject matter appealed to a very specific niche. She said she expected steady sales from the "daytimer" market—those customers who hung out in bookstores, reading and browsing. She said they would discover my book eventually and sales would pick up. Their friends would see my book in their friends' homes, and reviews would be posted online. It would happen for me, she said. She told me that she believed in me, and told me that I should, too.

I obsessively checked the reviews. The few that I could find were mildly enthusiastic, but sales continued to trickle in. There was no way the advance was going to sustain me for long, and the royalties from other sources were just barely stocking my fridge. I decided to go through my contacts and dig up some freelance work. It was June, and there were always weddings that needed photographers. I gave Todd a call.

Late that next August, I had a burst in sales. By mid-September, five hundred copies had sold in one week.

"See?" my agent said. "I told you it would happen for you. I had three calls from magazines asking for the rights to reprint the cover photo."

That night, I dreamt about the carnival again. This time, after I reached for the lens cap, the camera strap snagged on the carousel and I was sucked under it. Trying to claw my way out, I smacked my hand on the bedside table and woke up.

Todd called me about a wedding gig and I mentioned my spike in sales.

"Maybe it's because of that kid who died," Todd said.

"What kid?" I asked.

A teenaged boy had died on a carnival ride in Maryland. I had to dig out the model-release form to confirm his name. It was the boy I had photographed at the ring toss. He was the cover photo to my book.

My thesis had proven itself true. The carnival was an active ritual space, and every ritual needs some kind of sacrifice. That boy on the cover had become a sacrifice to the carnival, and my sales spiked because of it.

Angela called me later that week to schedule a book signing. She said demand for my book was exploding. She said I had finally made it. She wanted to know what my next project would be.

SELTZER AND BLOW
Liam Sweeney

Digger heard his answering machine go off as he shifted the groceries from his left hand to his right, racing for the keys when the caller had a hundred-meter head start. He knew it was Mrs. Martin, and she was about to get the easy way out. He damned near splintered the door running in, didn't occur to him that the dog would make it an obstacle course. He missed hitting the dog, but he didn't miss hitting the bare floor, and neither did his groceries. His wits returned in time to feel the milk soak his side and hear Mrs. Martin say, "I hope it's no bother. Keep the deposit. Thank you."

He got up, dusted himself off and unbuttoned his now soaked white dress shirt. He looked down and purveyed the damage. The eggs were a coating of slime on the throw rug, and Brutus was licking up the milk, ignoring the small stream that was heading for the refrigerator. Digger navigated the groceries and found a dishrag to throw at the milk. Brutus whined.

"Go eat the eggs, ya' big baby." The button on the machine flashed slow red meaning one missed call; any more, and it would've been a fast red. Digger punched it twice to clear the machine. He could guess at what lame excuse she had for cancelling out on him. They hired clowns for their kids knowing they hated clowns when they were kids, just to brag to the neighbors about how special it was to have a clown in addition to the princess and the pony. It wasn't keeping up with the Joneses any more, it was keeping up with the cryogenically frozen corpse of Walt Disney.

He picked up the undamaged groceries, everything but the milk and eggs he went to the store for in the first place, and tossed the throw in the washer, along with his button down. Brutus walked around, frozen in his beggar's face until Digger tossed him a few pieces of ham from his depleting tray of cold cuts. Brutus, sensing the end of the gravy train, trotted off into the bedroom. Digger grabbed a Beast Ice from the fridge and settled into his recliner, resting his calves on the footrest. He grabbed an unopened fortune cookie from the TV tray, tucked in between the travel pack of tissues and three iffy AA batteries. He cracked it open and popped one end in his mouth, only to spit it back out in his palm. He unfurled the fortune. The only thing we know about future developments is that they will develop.

Digger sighed. "A shitty fortune, for a shitty cookie, for a shitty day." He turned on the television. Judge Gary was "The Hangin' Judge," made plain to see by the ten-gallon Stetson he wore on the bench. Digger wasn't even sure if that was legal, but the Brits wore powdered wigs, so what the hell did he know? Only times he'd been in front of a judge was for drunk and disorderly and public urination, and he was so glad they didn't give him sex offender on that last charge, he wouldn't have remembered, or cared, if the judge was sporting a jester's hat behind the bench. He was about to turn up the volume when his bicycle horn ringtone went off. Randy.

He answered, said, "So that's why I've been havin' shit luck today. Randy-fuckin'-Joyce."

"Yeah, hello to you too. You get gum on one of them big fat shoes?"

"You are a bad penny, kid. What do you want?"

"I can't talk to my sponsor anymore?"

Digger laughed, "That horse left the barn. I got a beer in my hand right now."

"It's never too late, Dig."

"It's too late today. Try tomorrow, but you better call early." Digger took a quiet sip. "Actually, don't call early. I know you're not calling me to save my heathen soul. What's up?"

Digger heard a belch at the other end, followed by coughing. Then Randy said, "Got a job for you. Something in your wheelhouse. Just hear me out though."

"So, a clown job, you're saying."

"Yeah, a clown job. I don't need my hedges trimmed." Digger was a landscaper before he got dry the first time and took up the red nose.

"There's other clowns, you wanna bust my balls."

"No, for real, look. It's a money gig. Not suburban mom money either, is that a thing with you guys, 'suburban mom money'? Anyways, it's not scrub money."

"How do you know what 'scrub money' is to me?"

"Digger, I been to your house. I'll shut up if you're sippin' on a Heineken and not a Beast Ice right now."

Digger pinched the bridge of his nose. "Go on. Where's this job?"

"Westhampton Beach."

"Aw, man, I don't know if I got the get-up right now to swing a Hamptons gig. How old's the kid?"

"That's just it," Randy said. "It's not a kid. It's this dude. He's throwing some kind of thing, and he wants clowns, lots of them."

"To do what?"

"I don't know…clown shit."

"Clown shit." Digger let out an exasperated breath. "You've got no clue what I do. You know I went to college for this?"

"Did you haze people with seltzer keg-stands? No, I'll stop, I'm sorry. About this job—"

"You know, I think I'm gonna pass."

"It pays five grand for one day."

"It what?"

"Five grand. That's a lot of rent and bills. And Heineken."

Randy was an asshole. But he was right about the money, and a Heineken would taste great right about then.

"Alright, fine. You tell me where. And there better be a deposit. I'm not getting stiffed at somebody's door in Westhampton."

"I'll call him. And oh, he needs, like, a bunch of clowns. You got any buddies from the gig?"

Digger picked up the can. "Yeah. A couple."

"Let 'em know. Same price, unless you want a cut, then, whatever you want to give them." Randy chuckled. "Y'all could show up in a Smart Car."

"Fuck you. Call me back." Digger hit end call and turned the volume up on cowboy justice.

The pot had grown to a hair over a hundred in ones and fives, big money for the Giggles Factory, what they affectionately called Johnny Ewing's basement. Shannon told him to keep his shit down there, said she was tired of putting her palm down in his makeup when she was putting on her eyebrows. Johnny had a poor man's dressing room in the corner, with a vanity, a rack filled with costumes on coat-hangers and a stack of boxes filled with props. But, as per Saturday night custom, Johnny was Giggles himself, made up, as they all were. Coming to poker night in costume traced back to the years when they were all getting there from gigs that afternoon. As that became less and less the case, they took it to be a ritual to the gods of the big top.

"Raise y'all five." Blinky threw a fin on the pile. ChooChoo groaned.

"Got kids to feed. Fold."

"You could always play beer maid."

ChooChoo's perpetual smile turned sneer and he squinted. "You're hilarious, Blink."

"That's what they pay me for."

"I'll bet five bucks you didn't come from a job today."

"Give me your money."

"A clown job," ChooChoo said.

"You didn't say that."

A hundred hit the table. "See you, raise you, what, ninety-five?"

Everyone's eyes widened as they watched Digger rapping his fingers rhythmically against the Formica table. One by one they folded. He scooped the pot into his arms.

"So we gonna talk about what I said or what?"

Giggles gathered the cards and started shuffling. "I don't know, Dig'. Sounds too good to be true."

"So now what does this guy want us to do?" Blinky asked. "You said it ain't kids, right? Did you even talk to him, or are we all going on the word of that punk poser, Randy?"

"Look, I talked to him. I got five grand in the bank right now, my deposit, and one for each of you if you're all up for it. He said he's having a farewell party, and the guy they're sending off is some big to-do, one-percenter type. He wants us to just stand in the background doing, you know, clown shit."

"Clown shit?" Whiskers raised his ridiculously painted eyebrow. "What exactly is 'clown shit'?"

"I don't know, I mean, I didn't ask him. Didn't wanna come off like we don't know what we do, okay?" Digger threw in a dollar ante. "I mean, five grand for a day's work. I'll fill my pockets with banana peels and do slip and slides all over his kitchen floor for five Gs."

ChooChoo said, "Fuck it, I ain't doing anything Saturday. You can get me that deposit this week, then?"

"I got checks in my pocket." Digger pulled out one of the checks and a giant peacock feather pen. He scribbled out ChooChoo's real name and passed it over. ChooChoo picked it up and held it to the light.

"My God, it's not a fake check," he said. "Just checking.

Checking, get it?"

Giggles slapped his knee, mocking ChooChoo's wit. "It's your turn, genius," he said.

ChooChoo picked his cards up off the table and grabbed his cigar from the ashtray. He lit it back up. "So, fellas, we gonna be a comedy team next weekend? Whiskers? Blink? Giggles? What say?"

"You said it's all day, right?" Whiskers said. "So, are we doing bits? What kind can we do that'll go on a whole day? You can only make so many balloon sculptures before people get pissed. They're gonna want physical comedy. Look guys, five thousand is a lot, I'll admit, but we're going to have to get together this week and rehearse."

"So?"

"So it ain't five thousand for just one day."

"Okay, so one day plus prep," Digger said. "You think they make five grand a night in the big top and get paid practice?"

ChooChoo laughed. "Whiskers is getting soft from the kid parties, where he ain't gotta do nothing 'cept watch the brats chase each other around the yard."

"Hey, I had a kid take an honest shit in my hat the other day, ya sonofabitch. Okay, fine, I'm in. Cut me that check."

Digger whipped out his feathery cash dispenser and Whiskers got his deposit.

"Blinky, Giggles, I can't make you go, but we can use the help. And I'd rather not return money if I don't have to. It's just one day. And it sounds kind of fun. I didn't tell any of you, but we're not the only ones in costume. This guy's like a big kid, I think."

"I'll bet. He wants clowns."

"He wants, and I'm quoting here, 'clowns, pirates, cowboys and hookers.' Hell, he asked me if I knew any pirates."

"Do you?" Blinky asked.

"No, of course not. But this is going to wind up being one of those crazy gigs we'll tell our grandkids about."

"Or they'll have a gladiator pit in the backyard and we'll be running from a lion." Giggles said.

"Man, how do you book yourself as a happy hobo?" ChooChoo let cigar smoke shroud his face. "You know, you can fake a smile with your mouth, but never with your eyes. I read that."

"Guys, I need to know. I gotta call this guy tonight. Is it three or is it five?"

"What kind of grown-ass man wants clowns at his party?" Giggles said. "Clowns and hookers?"

"...and cowboys and pirates, don't forget..."

"Yeah, that too."

"So the guy's weird," Digger said. "You're sitting around a poker table in your basement wearing red, glittery, size-a-hundred shoes. You sure you want to saw at that branch?"

ChooChoo held his forehead in his palm. "You guys stressing over a rich guy party and maybe what, catch a pie in the face? Get laughed at, and not in the good way?" He puffed on his cigar twice, the cherry lit up his face. "Last summer, it was slow too, this gig was. I ended up fixing septic tanks for a month. Standing in shit, human shit and piss, breathing in the fumes in a hundred degrees, 'cause it gets hot in the tank. Did it for a whole week." He held up the check. "I made less than this."

He tossed two cards. "I love what we do, but I'm tired of having to chase Mommy around for a hundred fifty after her kid spent the afternoon pinning the tail on my nuts. I'm gonna take this. If you two were smart, you'd take it too."

Giggles and Blinky had a conversation with their gestures. They worked a lot of team acts. Digger knew if one was in, they both would be in, and they'd all be able to show up in his sister's VW Beetle with at least a little bit of spectacle.

"I still think it smells," Giggles said. "But we'll hold our noses for ten grand. We're in."

They drove over Moriches Bay on Jessup Street and turned left onto Dune Road. It was a long ride. Clown cars, real clown cars, are illusions, false bottoms and the like. Packing even just five clowns in full get-up in a Beetle was about as comfortable as the overhead compartments in an economy airline. The car reeked of the smell of dry-cleaning, cigarette smoke and greasepaint. Blinky held the GPS in his hand in the passenger seat.

"We're coming up on it now, Digger." He knocked on the window with his knuckle. "I think it's that one right there."

Digger's eyes swept over the sculpted yard before he got a good look at the house. It was massive, all gables, porches and balconies, with dark gray stone facing and enough shingles to cover his block in Brooklyn. There was a long, circular driveway, but judging by the de facto parking lot on the side lawn, it might have been mostly decorative. Shiny, vintage sports cars were parked on the grass with muddy, road-beaten pickup trucks and SUVs with oval ski and marathon stickers. And, to the surprise of everybody in the Beetle, a man in western gear hopped out of another, newer pickup with a horse trailer and opened it up. They caught sight of a horse's tail whipping in the wind before they drove past it to check the house number on the mailbox.

"Yup. Eighty-three. This is us." Blinky pointed to the driveway and Digger made the turn. The sand dunes behind the house were low and the grasses sparse, the ocean beyond them calm. He lit the cigarette that he'd promised himself he wouldn't, knowing his sister would bitch about smoke in the car. As they got closer to the house, he noticed people on the porch. Men dressed in Goodwill were talking to women in cocktail dresses. A woman in fishnet stockings and a tight red skirt was laughing and pawing at a guy dressed in eighteenth century frills, high leather boots and a beaten down black tricorn hat.

"Will you look at this?" ChooChoo said.

Blinky let out a quick laugh. "Looks like they got a hooker

and a pirate."

"And a cowboy," Whiskers said.

They drove up to the front. Digger turned the key. "Show time."

Aside from the fact that packing a clown car usually involved illusions and trickery, getting out of a clown car, in any case, was a performance act. They got out, bumped into each other, tried to help each other in just such a way as to be no help at all, and managed to make themselves look like they couldn't help but fall over each other, all the while seeming as if they were continually streaming out. They did this by getting out the house-facing door and slinking over to the opposite door to get back in, only to get back out again. By the time they finished the gag, they had a small crowd of misfits watching.

A kid in a red vest came up. "Can I, umm, have your keys?"

Digger passed over the keys. Then he heard, "Great! Send in the clowns." He and the crew turned to see a man walk up, portly, with a patchy beard, sweaty matted hair and a white dress shirt unbuttoned halfway to reveal dark stubble. He sniffed. He didn't have a cold.

"Guys, looking sharp." He put his arms around Digger and Whiskers, and squeezed Digger's nose. Christ, Digger thought, not this shit all day. "I'm Danny. I'm the guy that runs the show. I'll take you around."

They walked through the foyer and into the living- and dining room combo. The place was done minimalist, clean, nothing ornate or personal, no family keepsakes, with generic modern art on the walls. It reminded Digger of the houses of Miami drug kingpins in the movies. He might be on the nose with the host there, but he couldn't remember seeing a kingpin's set-up that had a centerpiece like the one in this house; a coffin, gleaming rose gold with silver trim, silver swingbar handles, and a white quilted velvet interior, not counting the peacefully resting body of a thin man with long blond hair and a sharp nose, dressed in a suit that probably cost more that every costume

Digger ever owned.

There were seven people dressed in black, seemed like they were of all walks, but they were shaken up, some of them holding back sobs, some of them not bothering, blubbering like children. One guy was even slumped over, pounding the casket with his fist.

"That's Noah," the guy said. "His party. I know what you're thinking, but this is all in his will. He wanted this." Danny snorted. "'Course he was high as fuck when he made out the will, but I don't think he gives a shit now."

"What about those people mourning?"

"They're paid. We just picked them up off the street, got 'em some clothes. Noah wanted that shit too."

Danny moved the group into the kitchen. "Okay, here's the rules. You guys are the clowns. You do your thing. People are gonna be fuckin' their brains out. You walk in on it, you do a bit, spray 'em with seltzer, do up a penis balloon, whatever. I ain't sayin' you gotta screw anyone, obviously, but shit has got to get weird today. In fact, that is your whole job; make shit even weirder than it already is.

"There's coke around. You can do the coke. You can smoke weed if you can find it. But no coke. Noah died from that shit, so if anyone sees it, you're out."

"We don't do smack," Digger said. "No one does anything heavier than drink. And a doob once in a while."

"Drink! God yes, drink. Drunk clowns are the best." Danny said. "And the house is yours. Except the second floor. No one goes up there. Noah's pops has cancer, and he's good if I pill him up every two hours, but I can't do that if some damn clown or pirate goes up and steals the pills.

"So, go everywhere, play with yourselves, play with others, and if anyone gives you shit, you bring it to me. I'll pay you before you leave. Cash good?"

***

Digger was in the kitchen, filling up the bulb for his flower. He wasn't finished squirting the hooker on the veranda. She couldn't stop laughing and there were three pirates going 'Arrgg.' He was high as rent in that neighborhood. One of those pirates, Captain Clayton, smoked a joint with him. He didn't normally toke, but he couldn't resist.

"It's special weed, matey," Clayton said. "Grown in a government lab. In Cambodia. They used it to torture people."

"How do you torture people with weed?"

"They strap ya down and make you watch movies. Sad movies. Sad, Cambodian movies." He had a giggling fit, which was contagious, because Digger caught it, and still bore a smile when he turned off the faucet.

He heard glass shattering. The house was taking a pounding. If Noah had wanted something everybody would remember, this was it. He turned just in time to dip out of the way of a professional mourner and a cowboy wrestling with each other, knocking holes in the sheetrock. He watched the performance of a lifetime from one of the hookers through the open bathroom door, her head buried in Danny's lap, his nose sprouting a coffee stirrer, vacuuming a fat line of what Digger guessed was coke off a small, mirror-polished silver tray. Danny looked out.

"Hoo! Seltzer us, man, get in here!"

Fuck it. Digger opened the fridge, which was loaded with alcohol, soda and seltzer, and not much else. He went to grab a bottle, but a silken-gloved hand shut the door. Whiskers.

Digger turned around to see the whole gang.

"Hey, fellas."

"No hey, we're outta here, Dig."

"We didn't get paid yet," Digger said. "It's not long, it's calming down now. Just—"

"The fuck it is," Blinky said. "Are you high? Shit, you are."

"Just a bit. Look, we won't get paid."

"Make that motherfucker pay." Whiskers said. "I just got hit in the face with a pie. A real pie. Fucking apple, in a glass dish.

My eyes are burning, man."

"For real, Dig, I had one of those cowboy freaks try to ride me. All day."

"That comes with the job." Digger opened the fridge. "Wait, by 'ride you,' you mean—"

"Like a horse, what do you think I mean?" ChooChoo said. "And he did ride me. And I fucking knocked him out."

"What did Danny do?"

"That crazy-ass patted me on the back and put a hundred in my pocket."

"Well, shit, that's—"

"No, that's not good, not a part of the gig. Shit's getting dangerous. Everybody in this house is high as balls, including you, apparently."

Digger heard more crashing in the living room. Maybe the fellas had it right. He glanced over at the open bathroom door. Danny was wasted, and the hooker was trying to conjure up a serpent in his lap, and not having much of a go of it.

"Well, there's Danny. You think we'll get our money out of him right now?"

"Go ask him," Giggles said. "You know, when he's done."

"Nah, he's got coke dick, ask him now," Whiskers said.

Digger grabbed the seltzer and went into the bathroom. He checked Danny's tray; empty. Danny bobbed his head up and down like a giddy kid, and Digger went to Seltzer Town, even spraying himself for good measure.

"Hey, Danny, it's getting crazy in here. We gotta go. What's up with pay?"

"I get it. It's adult time anyway. That big guy, dressed in black, looking over Noah and the coffin? He can cut you a check. He's the only sober guy here," he looked at Whiskers. "Except for, like, this guy." He laughed like the world was laughing with him.

Digger and the rest of the guys walked out into the living room, in search of the big man in black looking over Noah by the coffin. But the man in black was missing. And so was Noah, according to the empty coffin. A pirate was swashbuckling a very expensive vase in the corner, and getting the better of it. Digger patted him on the back.

"Do you know where the big guy went to? Or the body?"

"Arrgg, know nothin' about no big guy, but they took the body for a burial at sea."

"Are they putting it on a boat?"

"Arrgg, no. They found the clown car."

Digger grabbed the pirate by the shoulders. "A VW Beetle?"

"Aye."

"Where are they?"

"Out back, all of them. By the dunes. I stayed behind to keep the Royal Navy at bay, arrgg!"

Digger and Whiskers were the most in-shape of the group, but ChooChoo, Blinky and Giggles weren't far behind. The dunes separated the house from the ocean, but there was a natural break. They were about thirty yards out when they heard a commotion and the sound of a tire not finding purchase in the sand.

"Heave, ho." The crowd shouted. They were at the back, and on each side of the Beetle, trying to push it into a surf that was climbing up the beach. There was a man in the passenger seat— a man that kept flopping out. The big man in black, apparently not a sober person at the house, was jamming a stick at the accelerator.

"Hey!" Digger said. "What the fuck? That's our car. Stop!"

The crowd looked back, and quiet laughter grew to uproarious laughter. One of the pirates held a harpoon gun he must've found somewhere inside.

"Send in the clowns!" he said.

"No, no clowning, we want our car back. Party's over."

The crowd mumbled to itself. Digger looked at his crew. "Okay, so you guys were right," he said.

"Send in the clowns—send in the clowns—send in the clowns."

The crowd backed off the bumper and the side doors, making their way toward Digger and his friends. Digger took a guess at how long it would take to get to the road.

"Run," he said.

They stood outside as they waited for the cab to pick them up. They didn't stop running until they were past the bay, and they kept walking after that until they reached Main Street in the village of Westhampton. They were shoeless, each of them having realized that they wouldn't outrun the crowd in the sand in giant floppy shoes. Enough sweat had made their greasepaint slimy; add to that a quick pop-up shower that succeeded in soaking their costumes. They were lucky to get the coffees, as none of them could get in the shop without shoes.

Digger hung up the phone. "Cab will be here in twenty minutes."

"Did you get a hold of that Danny guy? About your car? Our pay?"

"Guy's out of his mind right now. I'm calling him tomorrow."

Digger leaned back against the fencepost and sipped his coffee. Whiskers had his hand to his face, cradling his jaw. There may have been a bruise from the pie dish, but it would've been covered up by makeup. ChooChoo rubbed his knuckles.

"Felt good blasting that cowboy though," he said. Digger pulled his wig off and ran his fingers through his sweat-soaked hair.

"Clown shit," he muttered.

CLOWN FACE
Richard Thomas

About an hour outside of Chicago, as you drive north toward Wisconsin, there is a man sitting in the basement of an old farmhouse, wringing his pale, white hands. In fact, his entire nude body is covered in a white dust, a powder, a singular tear running down his right cheek. His overweight body hangs in folds over the edges of his frame, the tiny, brown stool straining under the weight. There is a singular light bulb overhead, and it is doing a poor job illuminating the cold concrete, but maybe that's not such a bad thing. For the sake of this moment in time, let's call this man Bob—Bob the Clown. Aside from his chalky existence, the only clue to his occupation is a pile of clothes sitting at the bottom of the long, crooked steps. Let's look over there for a moment, away from the man hunched over in the darkness, and see what we have. A white ruffled top and pants, sit nicely folded, a hoop leaned up against the railing, and under it all a pair of black shoes—you know the kind—not just big, but ridiculously long, triple the size of a normal man's boot. But Bob is no normal man, no, sir. On top of the clothes is the only pop of color in the room—a red nose, and wig, made of rainbows. It's to be expected, these items, the melancholy that fills the space something that seems to haunt men of humor—comedians, and clowns—those that seek to entertain. Let's look back over at Bob now, and beyond, into the corner where there is a small, metal drain built into the floor, and overhead, a large shower head, looming like a giant, metal sunflower, dripping cold water to the floor. If we were to ask Bob what he's thinking about, it would most likely be the last series of shows—a circus up north, a festival out west, and even that cornfield downstate. They all blur together these days—the smell of manure and buttered popcorn, urine and cotton candy, hay and innocence. He wrings his hands again, and then stands up. Bob hobbles over to the corner, goosebumps rippling across his flesh, where he begins to wash off the cloud of white, his costume of the day, the way he is able to meander through any festive occasion with hardly a worry—balloons in hand, a smile on his face, knots twisting in his gut, blood filling his shoes. The water is freezing on his skin, and he runs his large, meaty hands over his soft, fleshy skin, sloughing the white onto the ground, closing his eyes as the water pours down over him, sobbing into the darkness. The more he rubs, the more he washes, the more Bob reveals. He turns in a circle, slowly, wiping, and washing, the floor turning white, as the tougher, grey skin reveals itself underneath, a mottled flesh rising to the surface, the concrete starting to accumulate other items—translucent scales, long sharp hairs, cracked, rotting fingernails, and square, browning teeth. No amount of sobbing will change this molting, this transformation, no amount of pleading, praying, or bartering. When he opens his eyes, searching for some sort of explanation, perhaps, some sort of forgiveness, his eyes turn a dull yellow, a sickness that fills his red, swollen eye sockets, spitting blood at his feet, as his mouth fills with razorblades. A whirlwind of voices stuffs his head, screams of children going up and down the rides, rollercoasters and spinning buckets, vendors hawking games and toys, the clink of plastic rings against glass milk bottles, the sounds of a band tuning up, guitars and the beat of a drum, a car honking at the edge of a parking lot, a door slamming shut with a dull thud, and names yelled out, Daddy, and then the pop of a balloon, the crying of somebody upset, a woman perhaps, maybe a girl, something spilled, somebody hurt, a person lost. Bob tries to breathe, and his chest fills with long, tangled bits of red and orange balloons, bending over, he vomits up pieces of corndog, funnel cake, fabric, and tiny bones. Finger bones, there are so many in the human hand—twenty-seven in total, spilling onto the hard, grey concrete like dice. Finally, he turns off the water, standing still in the quiet, avoiding the waning bulb that swings oh so gently in the cool, musty basement air, instead choosing to lurch toward the corner, and the darkness, squatting now in the shadows, eyes cast to the staircase. Bob is thinking of the future—a day, a week, a month down the road—when he knows he will find himself wandering down a midway, his skin covered in white dust, his hands kneading colorful rubber balloons, a smile drawn on his face, a red nose bright red in the center of his face, his wig a shining beacon of hope and promise, as his gut clenches, and his teeth elongate, all hidden behind the suit, and the shoes, and the laughter. Let's follow his gaze back over to the staircase, and even walk slowly up a bit, to the open door that spills just a bit of sunlight into the expanding darkness, and then out into the kitchen, a radio playing softly on the counter, a window open, the sound of birds chirping, the long grasses blowing in the wind, the corn and soybeans filling the fields for as far as the eye can see, to the grey minivan driving up the rock road, dust spilling behind it, shadows dancing in the clouds— lions cavorting, strongmen and bearded ladies, a top hat and tails, and of course, frolicking clowns—and the laughter spilling from the mother, and the boy, the girl, the dog yapping, sticking its head out the window. Bob trembles in the darkness, a large tin of powder and a pink puff waiting for him next to a long, crooked mirror that leans against the basement wall. Bob is hungry.

TOMMY'S BIRTHDAY
J.L. Abramo

When I was a few months shy of my thirteenth birthday, I was invited to Tommy Morea's thirteenth birthday party. Tommy had promised a big surprise. Johnny, Eddie and I tried to predict what was in store. Tommy's father owned and operated a very successful trash removal company, and he could afford to be extravagant.

"Maybe it's a pony," Johnny said.

"Or a ride," said Eddie.

A ride was an amusement park type ride that was portable—delivered by truck to the site of the festivities. A Ferris wheel, a pirate ship, a whip. The pirate ship was like a large boat that swung up and down on an axle. At its high point, the passengers were at nearly a ninety-degree angle to the ground twenty feet below. The whip was six two-seated cars on an oval track that violently whipped around its oval ends. We all favored the whip.

"Maybe it's a pony and a whip," I said, always the optimist.

When we arrived on bikes to Tommy's house we looked for signs. There was no truck on the street and no pony manure evident on the lawn. We were disappointed but hopeful.

After a three-legged race, which Eddie and I won handily, and a potato sack race, which left me with two scraped elbows, we were getting impatient.

Finally, Tommy's father announced that the big surprise would be revealed in twenty minutes. I decided I had time to tend to my wounds and went to find a bathroom.

The door was closed and—although since that time I always knock to be certain—I turned the knob, found the door un-locked, and pushed it open.

Talk about surprises.

The man stood in front of the bathroom sink, his back to me. He was big. He had a head of wild orange hair, a puffy purple shirt with big yellow polka dots, and matching pants that were down around his knees partially covering very large red shoes. Before he turned to me I caught his reflection in the mirror. A white painted face with a thick red outline around the mouth, and a good-sized red ball for a nose. When he did turn my way, I saw Tommy's mother propped on the edge of the sink with her legs in the air.

"Get out," the man said, "and if you tell anyone what you saw I will kill your whole family."

I quickly beat it.

I didn't take the threat seriously but, since I didn't really care what Mrs. Morea did in her spare time and I didn't want to ruin Tommy's big day, I decided to keep it quiet. The sight of the woman with her knees up above her shoulders and the man's creepy voice were unnerving and instilled in me an instant and lifelong dislike of clowns rivaled only by my distaste for raw green peppers or runny eggs, and my disenchantment with any cover of a Dylan song other than Jimi Hendrix's "All Along the Watchtower."

I decided to leave the party before Tommy's dad introduced the clown—who had been doing his wife—to a backyard packed with anxious adolescents.

I told Eddie and Johnny that my injuries were hurting badly and I needed the healing powers of my mother. They both knew better than to question my toughness. I peddled my Schwinn home, hoping that my father was not at the house to belittle me for being a clumsy good-for-nothing. For the hundredth time.

My mother applied the age-old remedy, mercurochrome, which burned like hell and left both elbows painted as orange as the wig on the man in Morea's bathroom.

Even at twelve years old I had heard stories of young people running off with the circus to escape what they perceived as a dead-end existence in a middle-of-nowhere Midwest town.

But, when Tommy's mother walked away from her family—a few weeks after Tommy's birthday party—that was a new one on me.

Frances Morea had left a short note.

I'm sorry. I'm not happy here. I need to go.

And she was never heard from again.

Tommy's father was devastated.

He had truly loved his wife, and her actions were as unexpected as snow in August.

He was left lonely, embarrassed, and bewildered.

And Mike Morea was totally unprepared for single parenthood.

The demands of building and running his business had left him little time for learning the nuances of child rearing. After his wife's abrupt departure, he threw himself entirely—body and mind—into his work. Becoming even further detached from his only child.

And clueless as to Tommy's needs.

Tommy was effectively orphaned.

A combination of our general goodwill—and more than a small amount of prompting from our mothers—persuaded Eddie Baretta, Johnny Sullivan and me to welcome Tommy into our tight little circle.

Tommy was not a great fit.

We were all sports fanatics. We religiously followed the Mets and the football Giants.

We all loved, played and knew baseball.

Tommy couldn't tell you the difference between a ground

rule double and the infield fly rule, on the playing field he was all thumbs, and at the plate he couldn't hit anything smaller than the broad side of a barn.

On top of that we were tough. Rather than avoiding confrontations with kids from other blocks, we invited and embraced them.

The Three Musketeers of West 10th Street, a title we didn't originate but gladly adopted, were respected from McDonald to Stillwell Avenues.

Tommy Morea was soft.

We drifted apart after high school—different colleges, different interests, time consuming girlfriends.

The last time I had seen Tommy was at Eddie's wedding.

Soon after, Eddie and his new bride left Brooklyn for Las Vegas—where they live with their three children and where Eddie has been very successful selling real estate. Eddie and I get together for a drink once or twice a year when he comes in to visit his parents or I go out there to play poker with the big boys.

John Sullivan is an NYPD detective out of the Seventieth Precinct in Midwood.

John and I see each other if and when he is willing to respond to one of my frequent calls for help. My work can often benefit from having an old friend inside the department—but John rarely has anything to gain from going out on a limb for me.

And Sullivan never lets me forget I owe him big time.

Those long-neglected memories of the party and the old gang revisited me moments after Tommy Morea called my office and insisted he had to see me as soon as possible.

A light rapping on my office door interrupted my trip down memory lane.

I called out that the door was open, and rose to meet my visitor.

Tommy Morea stepped into the room.

I met him halfway with my hand extended but, instead of

accepting the handshake, he took a quick step closer to me and gave me an awkward hug.

I offered him a seat across from mine at the antique table I used as a desk.

We both sat.

Tommy Morea hadn't changed much. He was a chubby kid at thirteen, a chubby twenty-six-year-old at Eddie's wedding, and a chubby thirty-six-year-old in the chair facing mine.

He was wringing his hands, looking as if he had absolutely no idea about how to begin a conversation.

I, on the other hand, could never be accused of being unable to get the ball rolling.

"So," I said.

"I think my mother was murdered."

Tommy's face told me he believed what he'd said, but it had come from out of left field.

I took a few moments before responding, and then tried to sound as if I didn't consider the suggestion absurd.

"Why would you think that? As I recall, your mother left home voluntarily."

"I was only thirteen and, as I'm sure you remember, very awkward and immature for my age. I could never understand why my mother would have simply walked away, or understood why we never heard a single word from her after she left. Until I saw this."

He reached into his pocket, removed a newspaper article, and handed it across the table.

I took a look.

A woman, Lorraine Gorman, had been found shot to death in her home the previous August.

Harold Gorman claimed he had left the house very early, his wife still asleep in bed, to mow the front lawn before it became unbearably hot outdoors.

After completing only half the job, the lawnmower ran out of gas.

Gorman drove to a service station, filled a gas can, came back to finish the work, and went back into the house.

Curious about why his wife was not yet up and about, he entered the bedroom where he found her body on the floor at the foot of the bed.

After determining his wife was dead, Gorman phoned the police. It appeared a lot like suicide—but without murder cases, homicide detectives would be out of a job.

So, as is customary in such instances, the husband was considered a person of interest.

Harold Gorman was charged in the murder of his wife.

He remained free, on bail, while prosecutors tried to build a case to present to a grand jury for indictment.

Gorman's defense was well thought out, and somewhat persuasive.

The weapon was registered to his wife, and Gorman claimed to have no knowledge of its existence.

There were no fingerprints on the weapon other than those of the victim.

According to Gorman, his wife had been unresponsive and depressed since having been diagnosed with breast cancer—faced with the probability of radical surgery.

The position of the woman's body, and the location of the weapon, were consistent with what would be expected had she put a gun to her head and pulled the trigger.

No neighbors came forward with reports of knock-down battles or outside love affairs.

The case developed by the prosecution was not as compelling.

They pointed to a life insurance policy held by the victim, which did not preclude death by suicide, as a conceivable motive.

There was the testimony of the victim's sister who swore under oath that Lorraine had been dealing courageously and optimistically with her illness—and insisted that, as a devout Catholic, Lorraine would never have considered suicide.

Finally, there was a record of a past complaint against Gorman for domestic abuse. A complaint that was later withdrawn.

It was not enough to convince the grand jury to indict, and charges were dropped.

End of story.

"Am I missing something here?" I asked, after quickly reading the article.

"Does Gorman appear innocent to you?"

"Not very, but neither did Simpson. That's our legal system, Tommy, innocent unless proven guilty. The prosecution couldn't sell their case and that, as they say, was that. But what does all of this have to do with your mother?"

"Look at his picture."

I turned my attention back to the newspaper article and studied the photograph of Harold Gorman.

It rang no bells.

"I recall you left early from my birthday party years ago," Tommy said, "but do you remember that my father had hired a clown?"

Unfortunately, I did.

"Yes."

"I saw him before he left, when my father was paying him. He had removed his costume and makeup," Tommy said. "He was much younger than in the newspaper photograph, but I am sure it is the same man."

I looked at the photograph again, trying to imagine Gorman in an orange wig and a big red nose.

What I saw instead was a pair of puffy purple pants with large yellow polka dots down around his knees.

"You think when your mother left, she ran away with the clown?"

"Yes," Tommy said. "And I believe the clown killed her."

I didn't know what to say, so for a while I said nothing.

Tommy Morea broke the silence.

"Nick."

"Have you considered going to the police?"

"Would you?"

I may have considered taking it to John Sullivan, but not without something a lot more concrete than Tommy's imagination.

"No," I had to admit.

"Can you help me?"

"Help you do what?"

"Find out what happened to my mother."

"I don't know, Tommy. I would like to—but if I can is another question. Give me a few days to try to work something out. Leave me a telephone number where I can reach you," I said, pushing a slip of paper and a pencil his way. "How did you find me?"

"Phone directory. Nick Ventura, Private Investigator. Who would have imagined?"

"Not me," I said. "I'll call you."

I devoted the remainder of the afternoon to another case, with the hope I could wrap it up by day's end.

The following morning, ignoring the voice in my head warning me against it, I turned my attention to Harold Gorman.

Harold Gorman was not difficult to find. I located an address and a telephone number.

Roseanna Napoli was the woman of my dreams.

Attractive, smart, funny, and she could cook up a storm.

I called Roseanna and asked if I could borrow Max.

Max was a medium-sized Chow-Shepherd mix with more personality than most of the people I knew.

"Going to try picking up girls at the dog park?" Roseanna asked.

"You know me better than that. I prefer the supermarket or the laundromat."

"In that case, unless you are planning to shop for food or wash your clothing, he is all yours."

***

Max and I drove out to Mill Basin, parked, and took a walk through the neighborhood.

Harold Gorman's house was fronted by a well-kept lawn.

On the northside was a paved drive, leading to the attached garage. North of the garage was a narrow side lawn leading to the fenced yard in back. The same pattern repeated all along the street, providing some distance between the homes—as opposed to the houses crammed up against each other in my neck of the woods.

We strolled down the alley that ran behind the houses. Each had a gated wood stockade fence along the alley, and each backyard was separated from its neighbors by the same fencing.

Getting into Gorman's place from the back was definitely the way to go.

All I needed to do was get Harold out of the house for a while.

Back at my office above the pizzeria, Max safely returned, I browsed the internet.

Harold Gorman was, for lack of a better term, a publicity hound.

Major print media and broadcast news had given little attention to the case of Lorraine Gorman, and only at the time of her death and nine months after when the charges against her husband were dropped. But during the time Gorman was considered a suspect, free on bail, he missed no opportunity to talk with reporters from small local news outlets—from *The Brooklyn Eagle* to *The Mill Basin Courier* to Brooklyn 12, a cable TV station covering news particular to the borough.

Since there was no financial compensation for such interviews; money would not have been Gorman's motivation.

I had to conclude that Harold simply liked the attention.

I felt confident that Gorman would consider an invitation for an interview with a major publication, with a two-thousand-dollar stipend thrown in for good measure, irresistible.

Maria Leone was smart, attractive, and charming.

When Maria wasn't helping her Aunt Carmella run the pizzeria below my office, she studied for her graduate degree at the John Jay School of Criminal Justice in Manhattan.

Maria assisted me with cases occasionally. She welcomed the opportunity for hands-on investigative work, and what I could afford to pay her covered the cost of a textbook or two.

She was perfectly suited to play the role of freelance journalist, but she would need credentials.

So, before I approached Maria with the proposal, I phoned Lefty Brenowitz.

Lefty agreed to meet me on the Coney Island Boardwalk.

Lefty was by far the most talented forger I had ever known. And, if that wasn't enough, he was also a cousin from my mother's side of the family.

We sat at a bench near the Aquarium.

"I need an authentic looking Press Card in the name of Maria Franklin."

"I'll need a photograph," Lefty said.

"No problem."

"What else?"

"Back issues of *New York Magazine* and *Esquire* including articles by Maria Franklin."

"Any particular subject?"

"Preferably pieces built around interviews."

"I'll need to substitute her name in the table of contents and in the byline of the piece itself, and substitute a short bio in the list of contributors."

"Can you do it?"

"Of course I can do it, but we're talking multiple pages in two separate magazines. It may take a few days."

"I need it as soon as possible. And, Lefty."

"Yes?"

"Please give my best to your mother. Esther has always been my favorite aunt."

"Get the photograph to me today. I'll have it all done for you tomorrow."

I met Maria at her apartment, picking up a prepaid disposable cell phone on my way over.

I explained, in some detail, what I was hoping she could do for me.

Maria agreed without hesitation, asking only if she could keep the doctored magazines when it was done.

She supplied me with a copy of her passport photo, and then she called Gorman.

I listened in. Maria was very convincing.

She arranged a meeting with Gorman for seven the following evening at the Milk and Honey Café, twenty minutes or so from Gorman's home. She said it would be a short meeting, no more than thirty minutes, just long enough to "get acquainted" and collect some information she would need to work up a feature article proposal to pitch to *The New York Times Magazine*.

"He sounded excited," Maria said, after completing the call.

"I'm not surprised. I'll get the ID and the magazines to you tomorrow afternoon."

"I'll be at the pizzeria until five, and then back here to change from my marinara sauce covered apron into my successful professional woman costume."

I ran the photograph over to Lefty on my way home.

Home was a houseboat docked in the waters of Sheepshead Bay, a stone's throw from Clemente's Maryland Crab House—

where I had made dinner reservations for two.

I had promised Roseanna the seafood of her choice as thanks for letting me borrow the pooch.

On the boat, I called Tommy Morea. I asked him to give me another day or two.

Tommy seemed to trust that I was doing the best I could.

I poured a double Jameson's, sat out on the deck, and waited for my dinner date to arrive.

The next evening, we sat in the parked car. Roseanna Napoli behind the wheel.

She had insisted on coming along, arguing that she could be both lookout and getaway driver—and when Roseanna had her mind set, there was no talking her down.

We watched Harold Gorman back his car out of the garage and the driveway, pull out onto the street, and drive off.

I looked at my wristwatch.

Six-thirty-five.

Maria said she could keep Gorman at the Milk and Honey Café for at least twenty minutes, and it would take him at least another twenty minutes to get back home.

That would make it seven-forty.

I could give myself close to an hour inside.

Roseanna drove around to the north end of the alley, dropped me off, and went to park nearby.

The back gate was latched, but not locked. Getting past the back-door lock was a cinch.

I wasn't exactly sure what I was looking for, but I knew the best place to begin looking.

I found Gorman's bedroom.

I went through all of the dresser drawers, and the drawer in the bedside table.

A wood chest sitting at the foot of the bed.

A few empty suitcases on the floor of the closet.

A heavy metal strongbox also sat on the closet floor.

I knew I wouldn't have enough time to get into the safe.

On the shelf above the hanging wardrobe, I found a shoe box tucked beneath a blanket.

I took the box out to the living room, set in on the coffee table, sat in the arm chair, and opened the box.

There were a number of photographs.

Wedding photographs, Gorman and a blushing bride. But not the same bride who had died in the house the previous August.

And a long-expired New Jersey driver's license. The name on the license was Anthony Sanders, but the face was Harold Gorman.

I pulled out my cell phone and took photos of the photos, and the license.

I replaced the shoe box.

I went out the back door, relocking it behind me.

I spotted Roseanna's car as I came out of the alley, walked over, and climbed in.

"Did you find anything?" she asked.

"Some things."

I really didn't want to bother John Sullivan.

I had gone to that well far too many times, and understood it was nearly dry.

I had no other option.

There was an officer at the Sixtieth Precinct who often helped me locate a name attached to a license plate, but the driver's license I discovered at Gorman's place was out-of-state, and a decade old.

"What do you need, Nick?" John said, in way of greeting.

"Maybe I'm just calling to say hello."

"What do you need?"

"I'm sending a photo to your cell phone."

Sullivan was silent for a minute, and then back on the line.

"What is it?"

"A driver's license."

"Nick, you must realize you are wasting my time."

"I was hoping you could get me some information on the guy."

"I would ask what your interest is, but I probably don't want to know."

"A favor for an old friend. Tommy Morea."

"Tommy Morea. I haven't seen or heard from Tommy since Eddie's wedding."

"Can you help?"

"You know how much I hate having to deal with New Jersey's finest."

"I do."

"Give me a few hours."

I thought about saying I owe you, John, but that would be like telling him the sky was blue or the Mets had no hope.

I thanked him, and left it at that.

John called two hours later.

Joan Sanders had been found dead, a single bullet to the head, at a heavily wooded area in Northern New Jersey nine years earlier. Just before dawn.

Detectives went to her home to notify family, if any.

Anthony Sanders came to the door in pajamas. Before giving him the news, they asked for his wife. He told them she had left town, a few days earlier, to visit a friend in Chicago.

Then they did break the news, and asked him to come in to identify the body. He said he could be at the morgue in an hour. He never arrived, and no one had seen or heard of him since.

"They took prints from the house," Sullivan said, "but have never been able to find a match. I have to admit, Nick. You've got me a little curious."

"Impatiently curious?"

"Are you asking me to wait?"

"Please."

"You owe me."

Maria's initial meeting with Gorman had gone well.

She had spread it on thick, and he ate it up.

After speaking with John Sullivan, I reached out to Maria once again.

Maria called Gorman, telling him *The Times* had contracted the story. She arranged a follow-up meeting, for that evening, to go over the particulars.

We chose a coffee shop less than ten minutes from Gorman's home. She would call him a few minutes before the meeting time to apologize for having to reschedule.

It would give me enough time to get into his house again.

And wait.

When Harold Gorman walked through the door connecting the garage to the house itself, I slapped him on the head with a vintage 1940s leather-covered Billy club given to me by my uncle Sal. It had once belonged to a Brooklyn cop, who carried it as he walked his beat in Coney Island, before he retired and later lost it to my uncle in a poker game.

It was a beautiful piece of work, and worked like a charm.

Knocking Gorman out cold.

We had pushed three chairs close together in the living room. We dragged Gorman into the room, tied him into one of the chairs, and gagged him with a dish towel.

Together, we managed to carry the metal safe from the bedroom closet and set it down at his feet.

When he finally opened his eyes, he found me and Tommy Morea sitting.

Watching him.

I held the club in my right hand, tapping it lightly into the palm of my left.

I stood up, and walked to him.

"If you raise your voice," I said. "I will hit you again, this time across the bridge of your nose."

I removed the gag, and returned to my seat.

"Who are you?" he asked.

"I think the more relevant question is who are you—Harold Gorman, Anthony Sanders, or Bozo?"

"I don't know what you are talking about."

"Sure, you do. Your fingerprints will match those of Anthony Sanders who, for nearly a decade, has been wanted for murdering his wife. I'll let the police sort it out. What I need you to do is get me into the safe."

"And if I don't, are you going to kill me?"

"Not right away."

I walked over and reminded him not to raise his voice. I smacked his right kneecap with the club, swinging for the fences. I was sure his cry could be heard clear across the street.

"That was a poor show of self-control," I said, and I hit the knee again.

This time, he did a much better job masking the pain.

"The safe."

Gorman gave me the three-number combination.

Tommy sat watching as I pulled the door open. He hadn't said a word.

There was cash, but it didn't interest me.

I pulled out a gun, which I guessed had been used to kill Joan Sanders.

And I pulled out an envelope.

The envelope contained photographs.

Photographs of woman. A different woman in each of six separate photos.

Some, I could identify.

Lorraine Gorman. Joan Sanders.

And Tommy's mother, Frances Morea, as I remembered her.

The thought that there had been at least six victims chilled me.

But what terrified me most, was a seventh photograph.

Harold Gorman or Anthony Sanders, or whoever this monster was, in the full costume and makeup of a clown.

I stood up, and handed the photographs to Tommy.

It was one of the most difficult things I have ever done.

Then, I went to look for a drink.

I found a bottle of scotch in a kitchen cabinet, poured four fingers, and knocked it down.

I poured another, and I made the phone call.

When I came back to the room, Tommy was standing—the photographs on the floor at his feet.

His eyes were fixed on Gorman.

I had seen similar looks in the eyes of witnesses to terrible accidents.

"Can I have some time with him alone?" Tommy asked.

"Sure. I'll wait outside. John Sullivan will be here soon."

I had placed the Billy club on top of the safe.

I thought for a moment about picking it up on my way out, but left it sitting there.

I walked out to the front porch and I lit a cigarette.

Sullivan's car rolled up to the front of the house ten minutes later.

"Well?"

"The suspect is roped and tied inside."

"Did this guy really kill Tommy's mother?"

"I have no doubts. Her and at least five other women. Tommy is in there with him."

"Do you think Tommy could kill the guy?"

"No, not Tommy. I could. Easily."

Tommy walked out of the house and joined us, carrying the leather-covered club.

John and Tommy greeted each other.

"Are you all right?" I asked, when Tommy handed the club to me.

"My mother told him she was going to leave him. She said she wanted to go back to her family. He couldn't talk her out of it. He drugged her, smothered her while she slept, drove her out to Plum Beach and buried her there."

"Did he say where at Plum Beach?" John asked.

"He couldn't remember. It was more than twenty years ago. With the crabs, fox and wild dogs out there, she's long gone."

"I need to take him in, lock him up in a cage, and call for a forensics team," John said, heading for the front door.

For a moment, I wondered if things might have turned out differently if—all those years ago—I had told Tommy or his father what I had seen in the bathroom.

I pushed the thought aside.

"I'm really sorry, Tommy."

"You have nothing to be sorry about, Nick. I'm thankful. I needed to know."

"Let's get out of here, I'll drive you home."

"I should go to see my father."

"No problem, I can take you there."

"Can we stop for something to eat first?"

"Sure. Italian?"

"Italian sounds good," Tommy said. "It's funny."

"What's that?" I asked, unable to imagine anything funny about anything.

"Today is my birthday."

"Well, how do you like that," I said. "I guess dinner is on me."

CLOWNS IN MY COFFEE
Grant Jerkins

"…where's the baby…Connor…wake up…where's Jeremy… where's the baby…"

The couch. It had looked so comfortable. And he had been so tired.

Connor could remember opening his eyes. It was the last time he ever felt good. He hadn't intended to fall asleep, but it had felt so satisfying and natural. So right. His son, Marcus, and his wife, Elsa, were both asleep. It was just him and his infant son, Jeremy, who were up. Everybody else was dreaming.

Jeremy had been colicky. A difficult baby. It seemed like all he did was cry. It was wearing Elsa out. She was a good mother. A good wife. Sometimes he called her Else for short. His Little Else. I need air to breathe, food to eat, and Little Else, he would say and she would smile. And it took on another meaning, too. In the bedroom at night he would say, to be a contented man, all I need is Elsa and Little Else, and she would blush and give herself to him. Little Else.

The new baby was wearing Elsa down. The crying. Jeremy was never content. He required constant attention. Demanded it. You could see Elsa dissipating. Deflating. She was mother to two children and little else. Dark smudges under her eyes like a coal miner. The skin high on her cheekbones grew thin and tight and took on an oily sheen. Even freshly scrubbed from the shower, her cheeks looked oily. A taught shine.

She was depressed. Connor was certain of it. Postpartum. You could tell. It seemed like she went deeper and deeper into herself every day. Every time Jeremy erupted with screeches, you could see her retreat deeper inside. There was nowhere else. And she said odd things sometimes. On his way out to get to the office the other morning, he'd given her hug. As he broke the embrace, she pulled him back, sniffing him.

"You smell different. New cologne?"

"I don't think so. Same stuff you gave me for Christmas."

"Hmmm. You smell green instead of yellow."

Green instead of yellow. What did that even mean? Something about the exchange felt unreal to him.

Marcus, their firstborn, was two. The terrible twos. He was into everything. Cabinets, drawers, and anything he could put in his mouth he did so. And he had a particular fascination with electrical outlets. He was constantly looking for things he could jam into them. The child-proof outlet covers were no match for him. All by himself, Marcus was a handful. Enough to fill any mother's life with nervous apprehension.

They shouldn't have had another baby so quick. It was too much. For Elsa, it was too much. Marcus needed her. Jeremy needed her. Connor needed her. And Little Else. It was too much. It would have been too much for anyone. They were feeding off her. Draining her dry.

The baby had been screaming that night. Literally screaming. It was a wonder one of the neighbors hadn't called the police. Colic could be like that. Jeremy was screaming as though he had been set on fire, and Elsa didn't even hear him. She slept right through it. Slept through her own flesh-and-blood howling in pain. What kind of mother could sleep through that? Connor knew there was no answer other than depression. Clinical depression. He read about it on the Internet. Postpartum depression. The women grew despondent. Indulged in self-harm. They took their own lives sometimes. And worse. They just…lost hope. Lashed out.

He tried to get her to go to the doctor, but she refused. Wouldn't admit anything was wrong. That she was not herself. Depressed.

"I'm a full-fledged mother now," she said. "I've birthed a family. Whatever dreams I had for myself are gone. Sometimes there are clowns in your coffee."

"What?"

"Life is hard. Sometimes there are clowns in your coffee. It's a lyric. From that song."

"What song?"

"You know. The one about being vain. 'You're so vain, you probably think this song is about you.' And she sings, 'I had some dreams, they were clowns in my coffee.' She was right. That's what dreams are. Clowns in your coffee."

"I don't think that's how it goes."

"Sure it does." She started humming, then singing, "…I had some dreams…they were clowns in my coffee, clowns in my coffee…"

"No," he said. "It's clouds. 'Clouds in my coffee.'"

"That's stupid. Clouds in your coffee is just cream. All I'm saying is life is hard. I accept that. I don't want to go to a doctor for happy pills. I won't take anything that could pass through my breast milk to Jeremy."

The thing was, a week later, she took Jeremy off the tit and started giving him dry formula she mixed in a shaker bottle. Connor didn't blame her, but it was out of character. She had done all this research about breastfeeding versus bottle feeding and proclaimed breastfed babies were the healthiest and the happiest. She breastfed Marcus well past twenty-four months, and now she denied her milk to her infant son who wasn't even a month old. And Connor was certain she still let Marcus take a nip whenever he wanted. She was showing favoritism to one child over another. Big healthy Marcus got to nestle and feed in the warmth of his mother's bosom while the pinched and sickly Jeremy got a bottle of dry formula mixed with tap water. And little else.

When he said something to her about the discrepancy, she looked him in the eye and said, "I thought that's what you wanted," and he had another one of those moments where a feeling of unreality washed over him. Was this really his life? Married to a neurotic woman who neglected her children and tried to deflect the responsibility of her own actions onto him? Clowns in my coffee, indeed.

So it had been Connor to get up with Jeremy that night. He grabbed the baby out of the bassinet and held him in a way that placed the infant's tiny body upside down, braced by Connor's forearm. A maternity nurse at the hospital had showed them how to do it. Something about the pressure calmed colicky babies. Sometimes it worked. Sometimes it didn't. That night it didn't. The baby's screams were piercing, they cut through Connor's head and touched some ancient receptor in his brain. No parent could deny the sound of their own child in pain. Connor looked back at Elsa lying in bed. She was snoring lightly and the skin across her cheekbones had that too-tight oily sheen, like she had rubbed night cream into them, but he knew she had not.

But there was something else about her cheeks. Lower, below the bones, the flesh itself was puffed out. Like a pouch. Like she had something in her mouth, tucked into both cheeks. It made her look like a chipmunk. Maybe she had a bad toothache and had stuffed cotton in there. He knew her bottom wisdom teeth bothered her sometimes. But he didn't smell any clove oil or camphor or any other medicinal odor. Maybe she had an infection and her lymph nodes were swollen.

But Connor knew it wasn't any of those things causing her cheeks to swell out. It wasn't a bad tooth and it wasn't the mumps. He knew what it was.

He closed the bedroom door and carried Jeremy on downstairs. Something about the repetitive jostling of the stairs set well with the baby and he quieted a bit. The screaming now came in intermittent shrieks instead of a continuous siren. It didn't seem possible something so tiny and fragile could make that much noise. The baby had cried so much his face was purple. Connor carried him up and down the stairs close to fifty round trips.

No, it wasn't gauze pads stuffed into his wife's cheeks.

On one of the rare occasions she got out of bed before noon, Connor had taken advantage of the opportunity to strip the bed of the sheets that smelled like her sour sweat and put on fresh linen. He was pulling the pillowcase off her pillow, turning it upside down to shake the pillow out, and all these little brown balls came tumbling out and rolled across the mattress. At first, he thought they were marbles, but they had no shine, no gloss to them. There was a hundred-or-more of them. Little spheres. Like marbles made from common clay. Exactly like that. They had an earthen quality to them. And a smell. They smelled like food, but no one food in particular. For lack of a better word, they smelled green.

He scooped a handful of them and carried them downstairs to where she was napping on the couch. He nudged her with his foot. It had gotten to where he didn't like to touch her with his bare hands anymore. He couldn't remember the last time she'd had a bath.

"Hey, Else, wake up."

She opened her eyes and looked up at him but didn't say anything.

"Do you have any idea what these are? I found them in your pillowcase."

She looked at the handful of gray pellet balls he held out to her. She considered them a long time, and he could tell she was making up her mind as to whether to construct a lie or tell the truth. He wished she had lied.

"It's just food."

"Food? What kind of food? Some kind of health food? Why do you keep it in—"

"It's saved food. I save a little bit from every meal."

"You what?"

"I store it in my cheeks and in bed at night I roll it into little balls to preserve it."

"You what? What? Preserve it?"

"I know it's kind of weird, but I think it's a mothering instinct. Kind of gone haywire, but maternal. An instinct. It wasn't something I planned out. It just kind of happened. One night after dinner I realized I had some chewed food stuck back in my cheeks and I reached my finger in to clear it out and I just rolled it up into a ball with my fingers and saved it. Then I started doing it on purpose. I would store a little bit from each meal and hold it in there."

Connor stared at her. The whole thing made him feel nauseous. It made him want to never eat again.

"It's for the little ones. It's just an instinct. I would never feed it to them. You know that."

It's for the little ones.

Connor walked away without further comment. Really, what was there to say? He was going to have to get her to a hospital.

It's for the little ones.

A maternal instinct gone haywire. Well he should fucking well say so. What kind of human being refuses their infant mother's milk, but makes little chewed-up food pellets for them like she was a squirrel getting set for a long winter? A mentally ill human being is the kind that engages in such behavior.

Connor went upstairs and put all those chewed-food balls in the trash and then washed his hands and sprayed the bed with disinfectant, thinking, this isn't real, this can't be real.

"...wake up...Connor...Connor...wake up...where is the baby? Connor, where is the baby..."

It was three in the morning and all those trips up and down the stairs had worn you out. Jeremy still wasn't quiet enough to be put down. But he was a lot better.

The couch looked so comfortable.

You should have just made a pot of coffee and stayed up with the baby. But there were clowns in the coffee and you were so tired. You needed to sleep. At work, they didn't care if you'd been up all night with a baby because your wife had depression with psychotic features and slept twenty hours a day and when she was awake she stored pre-chewed food in her cheeks so she could roll it into little balls later to preserve it for the little ones and told you the other day she thought the house had been bugged by the Democratic Party because she voted against them in the last election. That last election split the country, she said.

No, at work they didn't care about any of that. They didn't care if you had to get your two-year-old fed and mix dry formula for the baby and change soiled Huggies and get a diaper bag together and get both the boys to daycare where you were always the first one there before they had even turned on the lights and they knew you would be the last one there that night—after dark—to pick up your children and the lady would be mad at you for being so late but she never says anything, just gives you this dirty look.

No, at work they didn't care. They didn't care if your own life no longer seemed real to you. They just expected you to be there on time, fresh, clean-shaven, ready to shake hands, smile, make good eye contact, and sell to clients.

The couch looked so good.

Jeremy was quieting. Just little hiccups of angst. So you sat down on the couch, bouncing Jeremy on your knee.

Then you stretched out and put Jeremy on your chest. Right where he could hear your heartbeat. The sound of it soothed him. The nurse at the hospital said the sound of a beating heart would remind him of being in the womb.

***

"…Connor! What have you done? Connnnnnnor! What have you done? Oh my sweet Jesus. Connor…"

I could feel his little heartbeat, too. It felt so good, so natural. We just fell asleep together. That's all that happened. We just fell asleep.

When I woke up Elsa was beating on me and yelling where was the baby and I didn't know. I didn't know. We started looking for it. He must have crawled off somewhere, so we started looking. Under the couch and in the corners of the living room. Under the recliner. Except we both knew good and goddamn well that Jeremy hadn't started crawling yet. Not even close. He was far too young. And then Elsa was screaming. The howl of pain consumed her. She was screaming and little else. She was screaming and covering her mouth with her hand at the same time. I looked at what she was looking at. Jeremy was lodged down between the couch cushions like a misplaced remote control. Like loose change that had fallen out of somebody's pocket. And just as lifeless. Like something not even real. Like this thing that wasn't real and somehow got lost. Because it wasn't real. You know that, right? It couldn't be real. Such a tiny thing.

He was dead and crushed where I had rolled over on him.

I was so tired. I didn't mean it.

This place they brought me to isn't a prison. I'm not in trouble. Nobody blames me for what happened. They keep saying that over and over. It's not your fault. Nobody blames you. What they don't understand is that none of this is real.

I keep telling them. They don't understand. If someone could just acknowledge that none of this is real, then maybe I could calm down and move forward and get my life back together and go home and be a husband to my wife and a father to my son. I just need one person to confirm my suspicion that this isn't real. Then this so-called self-injurious behavior would stop.

They took away my shoelaces and belt and my wallet and pocket change (like loose change that had fallen out of somebody's pocket). But then I did something with my shirt—around my neck—and they took away my clothes, too. I just have this gown I wear.

Somebody's at the door all the time. Watching me. One-on-one observation.

I don't know. I don't know what happened. I was asleep. She was the one. She was the crazy one. I just want to die. Nobody should ever have to live with this much pain.

They took my gown away because I tried to swallow it.

I don't get to have visitors, but yesterday I saw Else out in the hallway, talking to the nurse. I could see her through the little window in the door. I was in here, naked, watching her out there. The skin over her cheekbones was stretched thin and had that oily sheen. And I could smell her out there. She was different. She smelled green instead of yellow.

I started banging on the door because I wanted to tell them it was Elsa who did it. That she is unstable and suffers from postpartum depression. She has clowns in her coffee. I started screaming and beating my forehead on the wire-reinforced glass. I looked up and Elsa was looking at me through the bloodspatter and I swear to God she smiled. I swear it. I know they listen to me in here. Monitor my thoughts. So they know it's true. They know I saw her smile.

After that head-banging episode, they put me in four-point restraints. They needn't have bothered. I've come to a realization. I'll never try to harm myself ever again. What I've come to realize is that if there is even a sliver of a chance that any of this could be real—even a 0.000000000001% of a chance—then death would be too good for me. Death would be a release from my pain. And I don't deserve that. I deserve to feel this pain every waking moment of my life. If any of this is real—and I'm pretty sure it's not—then that is what I would deserve.

The nurse comes in and feeds me. I chew it all up like a good boy. And every two hours she has to let me loose. A state regulation. But just one limb at a time. First my right leg for a few minutes. Then she clamps it back down and lets the left leg stretch a while. Then an arm. Like that.

After lunch I had my right arm free and she turned away from me for just a second and when she turned back she caught me doing something.

"Connor, what was that you were doing to your pillow?"

"Nothing."

"I thought I saw you doing something."

"No, ma'am."

"Let me see…"

She reached for my pillow, but I lashed out at her, my hand tight like a claw. I'm sorry to say I hurt her pretty bad. Later, I heard one of the other nurses say she needed over forty stitches. Because I hung on. I didn't mean to hurt her. It was purely an instinctual response. An instinct gone haywire.

Next thing I knew the room was full of attendants and nurses and they were trying to get the nurse I hurt out of there and stop the bleeding and I heard somebody say he has a standing order for IM Haldol PRN. They held me down and gave me the needle.

I had the pillow clutched to my chest and I was drifting off as the antipsychotic took effect and I could feel them take my pillow away from me and clamp my arm back down and I heard things fall out of the pillowcase and skitter onto the floor. You could hear them rolling across the tile and one of the attendants picked up one of the little balls and stared at it and said, "What in the fuck is that?"

Another attendant was lifting my upper lip, pinching it back with his gloved hand, and looking inside. Carefully probing. I heard him say, "And what is this shit in his mouth?"

I looked up, my eyes heavy-lidded, and mumbled, "It's for the little ones."

TWENTY-FOUR
Marietta Miles

April swiped a sparkle from her eyelash. Swished her hips to the left then swished them to the right. Slow down. She tapped her toes. Listening to the music oozing out of the tent behind her she tried to lose herself in the melody.

The costume wasn't hers. It belonged to one of the older girls. April wasn't yet a woman and had to move gently so as not to drop the heavy, skimpy get-up.

Working hard to be dramatic, she swept open the red velvet curtains, peeked through her fake lashes and turned to see the eager eyes of the men. She fought the urge to cross her arms and cover herself. She was not keen on attention. This was not her job.

She was filling in for Cleo the Harem Girl. Cleo, Cathy to the family, was laid up after laboring with her second baby. It was a long birth but she would be fine enough to get back to work. Soon, April hoped. Standing close to the passing patrons made April's skin crawl. She closed her eyes again, but kept the curtain wide.

The fractured queue stretched past the main tent and the elaborate signs announcing Klein's Comedy and Circus. The men, kicking up dust and cursing, smelled of liquor, smoke and sweat. They herded past April and stared straight ahead.

Inside, the platform was lit by lanterns and two ladies stood still in the middle of the stage. When the calliope grew louder and really picked up the pace the men pushed closer to the stage, like a flood. The dancing girls' slinky silver robes dropped to the floor.

A gasp sprang from the front row and the men hollered out, the sound ringing like a dinner bell. April stole a glance at her sister.

Claire, older than April by three years, couldn't see the audience in front of her because of the floodlights used at each corner. April was glad her sister was somehow blind to the sight. That way, Claire could just pretend to be a ballerina.

April closed the curtain after the last man was through. She hung her head, left the tent behind and walked to the wagon she and her sister shared.

"What's up, chicken butt?" She was hoisted up by her shoulders and thrown in the air. Jazz smiled at her and planted her back on the ground.

"Holy shit!" She laughed, no longer nervous to be on the dim midway alone. Jazz always made her feel better.

Just like her, he was born on the road. The son of an acrobat and a sledge driver. Jazz could have been the strong man, but he chose to run with the funnies. He liked to paint his face and go undercover.

When he was a child, he had a nasty run-in with a double boiler in the hot concessions tent. He never liked it when regular people looked at him after that.

"We're bringing the front tents down, now. I left you a little something special on your desk." He rustled April's soft hair and pretended to pull a coin from her ear. April mocked taking the coin and jumping for joy. "Don't you and I wish, little girl. Coins coming from our ears. Fuck, yeah."

April pretended to be shocked by his language. "See you at the yard when I'm done." She turned and ran. The carnival workers met at the close of every run, behind the dance tent.

She would head back after she changed and guzzled her treat.

Her friend limped in the opposite direction, each breath a labor. Sometimes, he acted every bit his sixty years. His days started early and they were always long, but, most times, he kept a pep in his step. "Enjoy your surprise." He called to her and his four-man crew fell in step behind him.

Once home, she busted inside, nearly falling over the make-shift step. On her small desk was a tall glass of lemonade. She usually worked late selling game tickets. By the time she was done with her day the fresh lemonade stand was closed and out of the day's allotment of lemons.

The old woman who ran it had to check her money in and clean out the tubs before heading down to the yard to meet with the rest of the troop. She didn't have time to make anything extra for April.

Hardly able to stand the wait, April pulled her ragged clothes roll from under the kip and unfolded a pair of soft pants, flannels, wool socks and a wool newsboy. Evelyn "Crab Girl" Monarch had a son about April's age. He was a norm. They were happy to share their clothes with April and her sister.

The first thing she removed from Cleo's prickly, uncomfortable costume was the veil. Once the veil was on the floor, next to her everyday clothes, April scratched and rubbed her fuzzy, red beard.

She took off her slip and nearly jumped into her trousers because it was getting chilly and she hadn't hooked up the fireplace floe, yet. Standing up, she looked at a near hanger and stared at Claire's strange looking undergarments and costumes. There weren't many times she felt lucky to have the thick, fuzzy hair on her face, but she'd rather that over men drooling and pawing.

Feeling better, like her old self, April started sipping. Satisfied, she jumped from the lorry and quickly made her way to the rest of the troop. She could see they were huddled around a fire can. Several of them leaned against the old, useless cannon. "Human Bullet" D'Amato, Daniel, had passed away the previous season but the cannon still had a purpose.

As April approached her friends she began to slow down. She felt fine knowing most of the locals were gone. This was the best part of the night, when the townies left them alone and the company could be themselves. April looked up to the sky and smiled.

"Watcha looking at, boy?" A red-faced little man stopped April in her tracks. "Seen you coming from the pretty red headed girl's place. You kin?" The man was a broken fifty, not much taller than April and smelled worse than the horses. He gripped her shirt and started to pick her up by the collar.

"Bet you could help get me close to that sweet little gash." He rubbed his free hand down the front of his pants. "Yup, when she's done dancing." He looked toward the cooch tent. "Make her dance fer me. On me." He cackled and spit. "I bet she smells good." He danced in place.

"You'd like that too, huh? Ya ugly little dawg!" The old man started rough-housing, smacking April on the back of the head. Kicked her backside. "Maybe you've already been there? Lucky." He shoved his gnarled hand between April's legs and pulled it away like he'd been burned by fire then he laughed even harder.

"Ooo hoooo what we got here?" He grabbed at April's breasts, laughing like a wild dog. Pulled her hair.

April shoved him out of her way and skirted behind the tents. The old man stumbled after her, wandering and tripping up. When he found the midway empty, no sign of April, he stumbled back to the crew quarters to wait for his fun.

Still shaking, April was gulping air and coughing when she settled next to the rest of the family, then shouldered her way close to Jazz. His fuzzy yellow wig was crumpled in his hands and the fake flowers he carried for the show were on the ground next to his big black work boots.

"What you nervous about, Peanut?" Jazz asked. He saw how frightened she was. His face was still colored white and charcoal rimmed his eyes. Bright red greasepaint melted and dripped from his cheeks. The younger clowns gathered around him, dressed as he was and waiting in the wings, but he stooped down to look her in the eyes.

"I'm okay." April answered. "I'm okay, Jazz." She nervously pulled on her beard. Shorty, the strong man and wagon driver, ran around the side of the tent.

"Alright everyone," he stopped in their midst. "Mr. Klein said it was fine. We made enough money this run."

Mr. Klein was owner and manager of the carnival. April could almost picture the bald-headed man counting his money and chomping on hard candy. He mostly stayed in his wagon and only spoke to Shorty. Klein didn't pay very well but he provided for the gang. He had a doctor just for the crew and had a nice park in Florida where they stayed during the winter. He didn't judge the family's way of doing things, either. Shorty took another deep breath.

"But we got to leave tonight. He says we can't wait till morning," he waved his hand in the direction of the owner's camper. "He says we've stayed too long."

"Well, alright." Jazz liked the news, despite the need to rush, and laughed out loud. Rubbed his hands together like men do before a big dinner.

The dancing girls emerged from their tent. The sound of the patrons leaving, meandering away from the carnival set a different kind of music.

Claire pulled her robe tightly against her figure as she walked quickly to join the group. The other dancer sat down to take off her high-heels. Claire stopped next to Shorty and he put his coat around her shoulders. Claire was holding her shoes and wore her old work boots.

"That's sweet. Thanks, Shorty." Claire smiled at him. He grinned and politely looked at his shoes. Claire, like Jazz and April, didn't typically like attention.

"I say," Jazz started. "Since April was sent in as ringer for the ladies tonight and all, we let her do the pickin." He put his blistered hands on April's shoulders and patted her gently. Everyone agreed.

Claire came over and gave her little sister a quick hug and kiss on the cheek. "Thanks for helping." She said. "Choose well." April loves how much she looks like their mother.

"Here ya go," Jazz handed April the buck knife he kept in his boot. The long black handle showed twenty-three small but deep divots and serious ware along the spine. "You tell us who it'll be."

April took the knife by the blade and flipped it so the handle landed in her palm with a satisfying smack. She had been spending her free mornings with Adele, the knife thrower.

She walked between the two tents that remained standing. At the midway, she looked away from the loud crowd of men leaving for home and searched to her right, amongst the carnies own caravans.

Leaning on the front steps of her trailer was the red-faced man and try as he might he could not seem to stand. Or sit. He was pulling at the door flaps, peering in, and grabbing at the blankets as he fell to the ground.

"That one." April pointed at him and whispered. The rest of the group followed her gaze. "Twenty-four."

Clyde had done one too many foot longs. Flat on the ground he rolled over, tried to sit up and then grabbed behind his knees, finally righting himself. His stomach tilted like one of the rides and he was sure he was about to throw up.

He didn't really know if it was the hot dogs or the green apple moonshine that made his belly angry. He had a lot of both. Didn't matter, he'd already put it all down and now it was all coming up. His mouth was filling with spit.

His good for nothing friends left him here by himself. His wife, Dora, was gonna be pissed so he was in no rush to get home. He could get himself together right here. Clyde broke into a sweat and dropped to the ground. He waited in the soft moonlight for the world to stop spinning.

Just ahead, not five feet away, Clyde eyed a strange play of darkness against a tent. He squinted and tried to figure if it was movement or matter. The shadow snuck closer.

The black form took breath, unfolded and became bigger, wider. A giant spider, with thick black and red legs. It scurried toward Clyde and he saw the long white face and the bloody gash of a mouth.

His stomach came up, moonshine and franks spilling on the dirt and splashing on his chin. The phantom before him moved faster, as if it were flying and he squealed like a stuck pig.

Not a spider. A clown. It smiled, presenting long yellow teeth then raised its pointer finger to its sticky lips. Clyde couldn't stop his screams and rough hands sprang from the darkness and forced him out and away.

A cool breeze broke over his body. He shivered at the sharp gusts cutting into his skin. Though his eyes were still closed, he knew that he was stark-naked. Exposed. Everything that he was, hanging in the world. Defenseless.

He raised his head, looked in front of him, and saw his clothes tossed on the ground, a woman with swollen red hands attempting to rifle through his pockets. She made an unhappy sound with her teeth and moved away, smiling and pointing at him while she walked.

Clyde gagged, tried to cover himself. He could feel his arms and legs throb as if they were broken or he had been beaten, but he couldn't make them work. Disabled.

Looking down, he saw he was bound to one of trailers with rope and belts. The bindings so tight his hands and feet were swollen and purple, like ticks on a dog. There was a cloth stuck in his mouth and secured with a leather horse bit.

A large fire roared before him. On the other side of the blaze were several of the fuck ugly freaks he had paid money to look and laugh at earlier. Here they were, joking and talking. Like people. They made him sick. His head hummed with hate, the veins under his skin strained.

He spied two huge men near the fire. As he watched them his hate shriveled away and reformed to terror. The white grease-paint was mottled gray. They had thick black gloves on as they stoked the gyrating flames. He choked on the hanky in his mouth and he couldn't catch his breath.

The cooch girls were there, fully dressed in overalls and flannels, and the little bearded weirdo was there, too. Clyde saw an old cannon pushed close to the fire, chase low and stretched across the pyre.

Flames licked the bottom of a cast iron pot dangling from the trunnion. Clyde's eyes were never any good but he couldn't mistake the oily bubbles popping on the surface.

Another clown, makeup half off and work boots instead of red shoes, shuffled past him humming a song under his breath. The carney dropped a sack of white feathers and stuffing on the ground near the two men working the fire.

Clyde's heart tightened then hammered against his chest. His entire body shivered and bucked, straining against his ties.

The bearded girl stood and walked toward him with the knife held forward. The biggest clown, giant arms carrying a pail of boiling gunk, edged around the fire pit, in a breath both were on him.

Clyde squeezed his eyes shut, waiting, and with the first black drop he spread his mouth wide. From behind his bit, he screamed like a man on fire.

FUNTIME WITH BLATZO
Ed Kurtz

If there were two things in all the world that Harold Bachterberg loathed to the degree that his blood ran hot with anger in their presence, they were children first and their awful parents second. Harold had no children of his own—at least none that he knew about—and for this he was exceedingly grateful. But the dozens of drooling, whining, pissing, shitting, bawling little bastards that comprised his mornings, Monday through Friday from 10 a.m. to 3 p.m. at the KPAT studio on the southeast side of town were more than enough to transform that gratitude into something approaching vomitous disgust blended with boiling rage. They filled the aluminum stands in front of him and to his left and right, shrieking and stinking, blowing diseased mucus from every orifice in their faces as their feckless mothers, already blown out on box wine and benzodiazepines, did little to acknowledge the vile little beasts, much less control them.

Harold Bachterberg hated every goddamned one of them, which made life more than a little challenging for his alter ego, Blatzo the Funtime Clown.

"Hey, kids," Harold bellowed, his chest tight and face slathered in greasepaint. "Who's excited for fun time with Blatzo?"

The routine called for him to jog up to the front center of the set, waving his arms as he went, but lately it was more of a dazed stagger. By way of response from the crowd, he heard an infant cry and a parent deeply sigh. Harold narrowed his eyes against the glare of the stage lights and, not for the first time, imagined that the heat he felt from them was in fact a raging fire that crawled over the stands, enveloping every living thing in the room including old Blatzo himself, and that the few who managed to make it to the doors found them barred from the outside, an insurance policy he'd thought up to make sure no one escaped. The fantasy brought a smile to his face, but it was only momentary. There was no fire, only bored children and their miserable, anesthetized parents, Stu at the camera and a couple of production assistants sagging in the wings.

Another day at the office.

And if Harold could keep from screaming until the hand puppets were up and he finally got a smoke break, he figured he could survive at least one more day.

He sucked at the filter of a mentholated 100 and squatted between a garbage can and the back door which he'd propped open with a crumpled beer can. Watching the smoke drift up from the end of his smoke, Harold thought again about the fire in his fantasy, the conflagration that would take out a significant chunk of his remaining audience and really make Blatzo famous. Only Harold didn't really want to be famous. All Harold really wanted was to be rid of the greasepaint and the wig and the stupid fucking red nose for good, but he'd been doing it for so long that he never managed to develop any useful, marketable skills, and without a steady paycheck coming his way every two weeks…

"Back in five, Blatzo," grunted a production assistant through the crack in the back door.

"Get fucked," said Blatzo.

The P.A. vanished, chuckling. Harold made a mental note to include him in the fire the next time he dreamed it up.

* * *

At Bull McCabe's on Seventh and Dixwell, Harold sipped a double rye and made a face, remembering the days when he could smoke in there, which always seemed to help it go down a little bit easier. The bartender, a stone-faced Irishman called Frank, eyeballed Harold from the far end of the bar. Frank didn't touch the stuff himself, which Harold knew perfectly well because they were in the same AA group together for the better part of a year.

Harold didn't meet the Irishman's judgmental gaze. Instead, he just downed the rest of the rye and said, "Set me up again, Frankie."

"Still got some white on you," said a voice in Harold's ear.

He groaned and slowly turned to find Lew Matisek looming over him. Lew was Blatzo too, in the Southern market. Occasionally they switched off or covered for one another for shows and appearances, Lew and Harold, though Harold hardly considered the other clown a friend.

Harold Bachterberg wasn't the kind of man who had friends.

"Right here," Lew said, gesturing at Harold's left ear. "Company property, that fucking paint. Somebody ought to report you."

"Hilarious," Harold grunted. He lifted his glass and balked, having forgotten it was empty. "Hey, Frankie. Come on, boyo. Help another mick out, will you?"

"Never met any mick called Bachterberg, you Polack gobshite," was Frank's response.

Harold couldn't help but laugh.

To Lew, he said, "Not supposed to even know my last name. Strict rules in the teetotaler club."

"What's he give you for your chips?" Lew asked.

"A heap of bullshit," Harold said.

Frank poured the rye and clunked it down on the bar before returning to his corner. Harold sipped, made another face. Lew sat down on the stool beside him.

"This how I find out I get shit-canned?" Harold said.

"That'd be news to me," said Lew. "Fact is, I come with a proposition for you, Harold."

Harold raised an eyebrow. Lew moved his eyes from Harold to Frank, and then back again.

"Let's hear it, then," Harold said, fishing his pack of menthols out his pocket. "But make it quick, I'm dying for a smoke."

"You go in with me on this," Lew said, "you'll be able to smoke all day long until those nasty things kill you. No more kiddos, no more mamas, no more Blatzo the fucking funtime clown."

Harold slid the pack back into his pocket.

The first person to see them was a portly woman in her fifties, her hair permed into a greasy-looking ball of moist fluff on her head. She smiled at them and put a hand to her mouth to cover a small laugh.

The second and third to notice were a younger couple. Neither of them laughed. The man scrunched up his nose and mouth. The woman just looked spooked.

Lew leaned in toward Harold and said, "Coulrophobia. Fear of clowns."

"I know what it fucking means," Harold growled.

By then, everyone else in line for the tellers at the First Members Federal Credit Union were openly staring at the two near identical clowns who'd just walked into the lobby. Bright blue hair shot out of both heads on either side, tapering to curling points. Their faces were white and oily, their eyes framed with large blue diamonds and their mouths expanded into massive, blood-red grins. Equally red balls perched on their noses, completing the tableau.

"Jesus Christ," the teller in the middle, a thin young man with wide eyes, said. "It's Blatzo."

"It's two Blatzos," someone said in line.

"Hey, kids," Lew Matisek said, his voice loud like he was on stage at the studio. "Who's excited for fun time with Blatzo?"

The permed woman giggled again, but she stopped the moment Harold produced the Smith & Wesson .40 from his colorful, baggy trousers and held it firmly in his white-gloved hand, pointed vaguely at the gathering.

"This is Mr. Handgun," Harold announced. "He's got a story he wants to tell you all, but Blatzo thinks it's better if we keep Mr. Handgun quiet for now, okay? And the best way to keep Mr. Handgun from telling you his story is to shut the fuck up and do everything Blatzo tells you."

The permed woman nodded rapidly. Most everyone else just gaped. The kid in the middle behind the tellers' counter looked like he was about to cry. Harold wondered if he'd just obliterated that kid's childhood with this scheme. Ultimately, he didn't really care. Nobody would think these two were the actual Blatzos, and that was the point. That was Lew's whole plan. Harold and Lew would be the least suspected of all.

Lew's weapon of choice was a Glock .45, which he pulled from of his own ridiculous pants. To Harold's eyes the guns were as indistinguishable and he and Lew were in their make-up and costumes, but then Harold didn't know one goddamn thing about guns. He'd never touched one in all his life before Lew put the Smith & Wesson in his hands the previous afternoon.

"Tellers one, two, and three," Lew announced. "Hands up where Blatzo can see them. Anybody gets wily with a silent alarm and it's going to get a lot more colorful in here. Clowns love color, you know. Particularly red."

Harold tightened up a bit at that. Lew had promised no violence. The guns were just for show. They weren't even loaded.

Point, threaten, grab the cash, and get the hell out, Lew had said. Seemed simple enough.

But things got considerably less simple when the permed woman shook her head and said, "Oh, Blatzo."

"Oh, shut up," Harold barked at her. "You think either one of us is the real Blatzo, you idiot?"

"He is," she said, pointing a trembling finger at Lew.

Harold looked to Lew. Lew looked back at him, puzzled.

"My nephews watch you in South Carolina," the woman explained. "I'd know that mole on your chin anywhere. Hell, even the greasepaint don't hide that."

Harold said, "Well, fuck."

Lew didn't say anything. He just pointed the Glock at the woman and squeezed the trigger.

A red mist burst from the big, dark hole that formed at her hairline in tandem with the deafening shot. Instinctively, Harold covered his ears and winced. A short, bald man behind the woman got spattered with blood and brain matter and started to scream. The woman's eyes rolled back into their sockets and she slumped dead to the floor.

"Goddamnit!" Harold shouted. "Goddamnit, goddamnit, goddamnit!"

Lew said, "Anybody else got anything to say about my mole?"

No one did.

The middle teller finally started to cry in earnest, and Harold couldn't blame him. He felt a bit like crying himself. All he'd wanted was to never have to set foot in KPAT again as long as he lived, to be shed of the people he had grown to loathe the most. He knew perfectly well a credit union would back up their customers, that none of them would really lose anything, and figured it was a fair enough deal for everyone once it was all said and done.

And here was Lew, blowing some lady's brains out with a gun that wasn't even supposed to be loaded.

"Come on, man," Lew hissed at him. "Stay in the game. It's time to collect, yeah?"

"R-right," Harold stammered.

From his ridiculous pants, he pulled out a long, green pillowcase and walked over to the weeping teller. He flopped the pillowcase down on the counter between them, pointed the Smith & Wesson at the blubbering kid with a trembling hand, and said, "Just fill it up."

"You-you mean with what we've got up here, or the vault, or-or what?"

"What's he saying?" Lew barked.

Harold said, "Just. Fill. It. Up."

"I-I met you when I was little," the teller said, his shoulders bouncing.

"Wasn't me, dumbass. Please hurry up."

Harold shot a glance back at Lew, who had started to pace. He only realized now how little he knew about the other Blatzo, and that the guy was most probably completely off his nut. And so was Harold, he figured, for falling so easily into this idiot scheme.

"You told me I could be a-anything I wan-wanted to be," the teller said.

Harold returned his attention to the kid.

"So you became a bank teller. Great, kid. Fill up the bag. I'm not fooling, okay?"

"I'm in college. I'm going to be an engineer. My dad never told me I could, but-but y-you did. You did."

"Oh, for Christ's sake," Harold groaned, unable to remember ever having said something inspirational to some kid, or to anyone at all, but his thoughts were scattered by the shot close to his ear.

The teller's mouth burst in a slurry of blood, saliva, and broken teeth as he let loose a horrific, gurgling yowl, threw both hands to his face, and dropped down behind the counter like a bag of apples. The tellers on either side of him shrieked, and they kept on shrieking until one of them passed out cold on the floor and the other's voice tapered off into a low croak.

Harold picked a shard of bloody tooth from his lower lip, flicked it on the floor, and turned slowly to face Lew behind him.

Lew Matisek was having a tough time of trying to contain his glee. His mouth stretched into a quivering grin and his round, alcoholic stomach pulsed with barely restrained laughter. He was, Harold realized, having a marvelous time.

Funtime with Blatzo, Harold thought grimly, as he raised the gun in his hand, aimed it point blank at Lew's face, and shot him in the eye.

The Pakistani guy at the liquor store laughed when he saw Harold, but Harold didn't really mind. He bought a fifth of bottom shelf bourbon and a pack of off-brand menthols, paid cash for them, and told the guy to keep the change.

A mild sprinkle was getting started when he climbed back into Lew's beater, an old Subaru hatchback that used to be baby blue, so Harold switched on the wipers and drove back to the studio. There still was no sign of police on his tail, which he found odd though not particularly satisfying. A quick glance at the digital clock in the dash told him it had only been six minutes since he walked out of the bank, empty handed, but it seemed to him like hours.

By the time he pulled up in the small, cracked lot behind KPAT, he could finally hear sirens in the middle distance. Would they know already where he'd gone? If not, they'd not be able to see Lew's shit-heap from the street. At any rate, they'd be along shortly. That was what the old contingency plan was for.

Stu was sitting in the aluminum stands in the shadows, most of the lights out for the day, eating a tuna fish sandwich out of a plastic baggie. He stopped mid-chew when Harold walked into the studio in full Blatzo regalia, the bottle of hooch dangling from one hand and blood spattering his face and costume.

After choking down his mouthful, Stu said, "Bachterberg? What's up, man?"

Harold continued to the stage, set the bourbon down on the floor in front of Storytime Farm portion of the set, and clumsily fished the Smith & Wesson out of his waistband. He held it aloft, not really pointing it at anything, and said, "Get on out of here, Stu. Tell anyone else that's left to go, too."

The cameraman's eyes bulged at the handgun, and without taking his eyes from it, he set the sandwich down on the seat plank beside him, rose to his feet, and walked briskly out of the room by way of the left wing.

Harold expelled a long sigh that seemed to deflate him, then walked with gun in hand to the right wing of the stage, behind which was the bank of lockers for talent and some crew. He twisted the dial on the lock, which KPAT made him buy for himself, and opened up the third locker from the left. His contingency plan, a plastic jug of no-name scotch filled to the neck with unleaded from the filling station two blocks from the studio, rested at the bottom of the locker.

He carried it back to the stage, set it down beside the bourbon, and regarded the pair of bottles for a long, silent moment. A door somewhere up front slammed shut, and after that, all was as quiet as could be. Harold had never heard such beautiful silence in the studio before. His fantasy, he was beginning to realize, was changing. There would be no screaming, shitting children, no doped-out housewives, no crew. He no longer wished harm upon anyone in the world apart from Blatzo the funtime clown.

"One down," he whispered, trying not to think too hard about the image of Lew's left eye bursting from the impact of the bullet he'd fired into it. "One to go."

Harold double-fisted it. With one hand, he hefted the bourbon up to his mouth to take a long swig, spilling booze down his chin and all over the ruffled front of his rainbow-colored costume. With the other hand, he spilled gasoline from the scotch bottle in a wide arc across the front of the stage. One for one, time and time again, until his throat burned and his vision blurred, and his nose wrinkled at the astringent odor of the gas coating the stage and the camera and much of himself.

He imagined he heard the sirens by now, but figured it was just that—his imagination. The soundstage was soundproofed and there would be no way he could hear activity out on the street, no matter how loud it was. Shrugging it off, he emptied the remainder of the scotch bottle gasoline right at his feet, then dug a smoke out of the pack in his pocket and jammed it between his lips.

"That wasn't fun at all, kids," he wheezed. "Sorry about that."

Harold Bachterberg flicked a plastic lighter, lighting first the cigarette, and then himself.

The last thing he thought before the fire overtook him, and the stage, and everything around him, was, I'm not angry anymore.

And that was nice.

GUT PUNCH
R. Daniel Lester

Clown was fucking with him today. First, rolled his ass out of bed at 7 a.m.. No need for an alarm clock with this mother on the job. Yelling in his ear, "AWWOOOGA! AWWWOOGA!"

"The fuck, Clown?" Easy asked, standing. Woozy.

"Early worm gets the best dirt, shithead," said Clown.

Easy yawned. Easy stretched. Easy flicked his right shoulder, sending Clown up into the air. Then, like a European football striker waits for the cross to come in from the wing, he timed it perfectly and kicked Clown headfirst into the wall. Easy heard the little bastard's neck crunch and it left a red smear down the chipped, yellowing paint. Clown flopped to the ground.

"Goal!" shouted Easy.

Clown gave him the finger. Tough as nails, no doubt. Easy had once clipped Clown's femoral with a boxcutter and he'd screamed and bled like a stuck pig all over the table. Then he did the backstroke in the pool of blood for a few minutes and when he was done with that Clown mooned him.

Clown raised his head, grinning through chipped teeth and split lip. His head was caved in on one side and an eye hung loose in the socket. As per his M.O., he'd crawl away and hide and an hour later return good as new.

"Sure," Clown said, "get your licks in now, asshole. But enjoy it while you can, today's gonna be a doozy."

"What's that supposed to mean?" asked Easy.

"You'll see."

"Cryptic little shit."

"Love you, too, Big Guy. Now go eat some cereal, you'll need your strength."

Tiny sold vials of stepped-on flake from an alley doorway off Main Street, under the cover of nothing because he was stupid, careless son-of-a-bitch with less sense than a mule that's been kicked in the head by another mule. But the clientele was strictly low-rent wastoids so Easy supposed the level of security fit the level of threat. He watched Tiny for a few minutes to see if anything in the idiot's routine had changed. It hadn't.

Over breakfast, Clown had bemoaned the sorry state of Easy's cash accounts and then said he heard Tiny was back in business. Five times in the last six months, Clown had Easy visit Tiny's pop-up store, for kicks and a quick injection of cashola. See, Tiny was exactly that and Easy was big, real big. But Easy kept it simple and plain. No sense reinventing the wheel. Time is money, after all. Like the other visits, today he strolled over, hands in his pockets, whistle, whistle, nothing to see here. Tiny didn't notice until Easy was behind him. Too busy wiping invisible dirt off his new Jordans.

"Morning, Tiny."

"Oh, hey, good—"

A fist in his gut doubled Tiny over, put him to his knees. Easy snaked a hand into the man's pocket, feeling for the vials tied up with elastic, as Tiny puked up his breakfast on the pavement.

"Damn, Tiny. Watch the shoes. They might not be as pretty as your Royals but still."

"Yulgeyurs."

"What? Speak up."

Tiny wiped his mouth and put his back up against the bricks.

His face was the colour of a poisoned sky, sick with clouds. "You'll get yours, Easy," he said.

Clown tsked tsked. "You gonna let him talk to you like that?"

Easy tipped up Tiny's chin with a finger, giving him the eye. "That right?"

"Well...I mean, you know. Karma."

"Karma don't scare me. Mrs. Kim's?"

"What?"

"Your breakfast."

"Yeah, daily special. Heuvos Rancheros."

"The tortillas, she make 'em herself?"

"The fuck do you care?"

And that was Tiny for you. Cowering on the ground next to a pile of his puke one minute, cocky the next, with nothing to back it up. It boggled the mind. "I don't," said Easy, "but maybe I make you eat them again to find out."

"Alright, alright. You got what you wanted, so..."

"So..." Daring him to say it.

"Maybe you could leave."

Easy grinned big. "Buddy, you don't want me around no more? I'm insulted."

"No, I mean—"

"Fuckin' with you, man. Don't get your panties in a bunch." Easy patted Tiny on the head and left him there in the doorway, spitting bile and tortilla.

At Mrs. Kim's, Easy passed Dex the bindles under the table, Dex handed back the cash.

Dex shook his head. "He'll shoot you one of these days."

"The day Tiny has the balls to do that is the day I piss green on St. Patty's."

"Still, he sells a good product. Not too stepped on, considering. But if he's an indie where's he re-up? And with who?"

"The fuck do we care?" said Clown.

"The fuck do we care?" said Easy.

Dex nodded. "True, I guess."

"Damn straight," said Clown, busy burrowing like a tick into the pile of baked beans on Easy's plate.

Easy sighed. "Come on, man."

"What?" said Dex.

"Nothin'," said Easy.

Clown first showed up when Easy turned fifteen. Woke up and there he was, lounging on his pillow. The world's strangest/ shittiest birthday present. Looked the spitting image of his great grandfather on his dad's side. Those old black and white photos his mom had shown him. Only thing she had of his father's.

"Wake up, fucknut," Clown said. "We got shit to do."

Shit, indeed. First thing he did was get Easy to lift a few twenties out of his grandma's purse. Easy didn't want to but Clown was persistent.

"C'mon," Clown said, "unpucker your shit shute and have some fun for once in this life."

Second thing was getting Easy to boost a chocolate milk from the corner store.

"But we have forty bucks," said Easy.

Clown shook his head. Mock disdain. "You're not thinking this through. We're gonna use the cash for hooch and cigarettes."

Third thing was convincing Easy to blow off football practice.

"Organized sports are for suckers."

"I like it," said Easy.

"What, the tight pants? The butt slaps?"

"Being part of a team. And I get to hit people and don't get in trouble."

"The hitting part I get. The rest is bullshit, trust me."

"I like Coach."

"Pfft. You think he gives a shit about you? Like, really? You're just a number on a chalkboard. A paycheque to keep his kiddies in diapers and formula.”

“I don't know.”

“Well, I do.”

“So you're the one lookin' out for me, is that it? Better than Coach. Better than Grandma?”

Clown tapped Easy in the middle of the chest. “Better believe it, buddy-boy. We're going right to the top, you and me.”

It was Big Mike that knocked on his door. After getting back from Mrs. Kim's diner, Clown told him to expect a visitor and to do what he said. Then Clown vamoosed, off to wherever he disappeared to sometimes. Easy stayed in all afternoon. Clown was a dick but his hunches were pretty spot on and it'd benefitted Easy in the past.

“You know who I am?” asked Big Mike.

“Yes,” said Easy.

“Good. So you know who I work for?”

“Yes.”

“Good. Well, he wants to talk to you.”

“Suppose I don't want to talk with him.”

“This is not really a door A or door B situation, kid. There's your door and how you're gonna walk out of it and into the nice shiny Lincoln Town Car downstairs.”

Easy considered it.

Big Mike smiled. “Suppose you see another way. I don't blame you for it. Maybe you're right. We could mix it up now and you're just big enough you might stand a chance. I heard you're pretty tough. Either way we're both gonna get hurt and then this affects your lovely grandma, too, you know? It's terrible when old people break a hip. They're just not the same afterward. But come with me, easy, like your name and I guarantee you, no one external to the situation gets hassled. It's between him and you.”

The Town Car was nice. Comfy seats. Sixties doo-wop on

the radio. Big Mike drove. Didn't take very long either. What surprised Easy was that the destination wasn't a sketchy warehouse off a dark alley on a dark street, but a two-car-garage-lots-of-SUVs-and-toys-on-the-lawn kind of neighbourhood. Quaint. Middle-class.

Easy followed Big Mike up the steps. Big Mike carried a brown paper bag he'd got out of the trunk. As they got to the door, Clown poked his head out the mail slot—"Heeeere's Clowny!"

Always the joker.

Clown wriggled through the slot, dropped to the ground, scaled Easy's leg like a lumberjack on a Poplar tree and climbed into the inside pocket of Easy's jacket. "There's a Chihuahua in there tryin' to make me his wife," he whispered, "so I'm hitchin' a ride on you."

Big Mike knocked. A thirty-something, fit, very attractive woman with a toddler on her hip opened the door. She smiled at Big Mike and gave Easy a look laced with venom.

"Hey, Mike. What's in the bag?"

"You don't want to know," said Big Mike.

"You're right, I don't. He's waiting downstairs."

"Thanks, Treen."

Big Mike nudged Easy into the house.

"That was Trina, the wife," Clown said, voice muffled inside the jacket. "The poop machine is the son. Talk about your May-December romances. I'm surprised the old geezer can get the rocket upright anymore let alone launch any astronauts into space."

"How do you know this?" asked Easy.

"Know what?" said Big Mike.

Easy did that sometimes, forgot he wasn't alone. "That this will stay between me and him."

"Nice save," said Clown.

Big Mike said, "He's many things, a liar is not one of them. Through the door there."

They went downstairs. The basement matched the upstairs. Plush, nicely furnished. Expensive. But upstairs had a feminine touch. Style. Martha Stewart with a fat budget. Downstairs was man cave. Giant TV and couch. Well-stocked bar. Pool table. And there was Tiny lining up a shot, purposefully not looking Easy's way as they walked by. Easy had never seen Tiny indoors and he seemed even smaller, less important, though clearly on his best behaviour. Shirt tucked in, hair slicked back. And it would've been a great moment for him, but of course Tiny missed the shot, cursing under his breath.

"Welcome to my home," said Henry Cimini, sitting on the couch, one leg casually over the other, looking very much the successful, aging entrepreneur instead of the drug empire boss he definitely was and the vicious murderer he was rumoured to be. "Have a seat."

Easy sat down. Big Mike took a plastic box out of the paper bag and placed it on the coffee table. He handed what was left in the bag to Tiny. Tiny grinned.

"I believe you two have met?" said Cimini. "William, aka 'Easy,' this is my wife's nephew, Marvin, aka 'Tiny.'"

"Oh yeah, we've met," said Tiny, giving Easy some eye-venom of his own.

"Right, hence our little chat. Tiny, I think you have something to prepare."

"Oh yeah." Another big grin.

"Give us a few minutes, okay? And for God's sakes, don't spill any."

Tiny nodded and went into another room. Easy heard the clinking of glass.

"Your wife's nephew, huh?" Easy asked. That fucking Clown. If he made it out of the basement alive, he would definitely be having a conversation with his "friend," one that involved an industrial-strength blender set to "puree." See if the little bastard could knit himself together after that.

"It's not common knowledge, but yes," said Cimini. "Not

her real nephew, something related to her first marriage but she loves the kid. Personally, I find him to be undersized in both the brain and brawns department but what are you gonna do? Family, even the not-blood kind, is family. Right, Mike?"

"Right," said Big Mike.

"So when he comes to me last year, begging for a piece of the pie, some territory, I tell him no way. I'd have to start him out street level, so he could learn the business, and it's too close for comfort. Too risky. But I got a lot of legitimate businesses so I set him up with something. Work your way to the top kind of thing. But that's not enough. Kids these days, they want the steak, perfectly cooked, medium rare, on the plate, cut up for them, all they got to do is eat. Figures because Trina's set, he should be too. Keep him in fancy sneakers and gold chains, I don't know what. So he starts skimming from some of my stash spots and selling on his own. And still I don't know about it. It's not until he comes crying to me about some big guy bullying him that I learn all the details." Cimini leaned forward, took a drink of water from the tumbler on the glass coffee table and then sat back. He nudged Big Mike. "This one's pretty cool under fire, eh?"

"He is that," said Big Mike.

"Maybe he's tryin' desperately to figure out what's comin'."

"Maybe."

"He won't, though."

"Probably not."

Easy's armpits dripped sweat.

Clown chimed in. "Stay cool, they're just tryin' to rattle you. If they were gonna blow your brains out, they'd have done it by now. And you wouldn't be in his house, believe me."

Easy said nothing, to anybody. He did wonder why Clown didn't come out of his pocket since he usually didn't hide in people's presence, but whatever. Plenty of other things to worry about. Like the sound coming from the other room. Someone, Easy assumed Tiny, was vomiting. Unmistakable. That retching sound, the splash of liquid.

"Okay, then," said Cimini, seemingly unfazed, "where was I? Right, my wife's idiot sorta-nephew and the guy he's having trouble with. Yeah, I find out he's been roughed up and had his stash, which is my stash, mind you, ripped off several times now only I'm just hearing about it because he was scared to tell me. Now, anybody else, they disappear, flat out, no question. I am not to be stolen from. But Trina'd be asking where he was at Christmas and family dinners and why he doesn't pick up the phone and that headache I just don't need. So I tell him, like any other bully, that what they respect is a show of force. And his eyes light up like that's exactly what he wanted and he asks for a piece. And I say, 'A piece of what?' Because no sorta-nephew of mine is going to go off half-cocked with a pistol and murder some guy in the street. Too much heat. Plus, knowing him, he'd miss."

As if on cue, Tiny stepped back in the room, carrying a tray with a glass, two milk bottles full of a chunky, yellow-brown liquid and several clothespins. He put the tray down and sat on the couch. Then he, Big Mike and Cimini reached for a clothespin and clipped it onto their nose. All that was left on the tray, the glass and two full milk bottles of something Easy didn't want to think about.

"Over to you, Tiny," said Cimini.

"With pleasure," said Tiny.

Easy felt Clown climb out of his pocket and squirm his way up his back and out his collar, hidden from view behind Easy's ample neck. "Okay, okay," said Clown. "I get it now. I just had to wait and see what the punishment was going to be. A little gut punch. Not so bad, considering. I thought they might break your leg or cut off a finger or something. Then we'd have a problem. But this is a breeze."

Tiny poured a glass of vomit.

"Kids these days," said Cimini. "They like to vomit, like a challenge. So Mike had a few of the bouncers at the club have a go. Plus, what Tiny contributed. Here are the rules: you drink one glass, every last drop and then we move on. Tiny has payback and you walk out of here, all forgotten. Except now you're on my radar. You're a big kid, can handle yourself. I got uses for that, you know?"

"Nod," said Clown.

Easy nodded.

"Bottoms up, then. And in case you need any last minute motivation, Mike show him what's in the plastic box."

Mike opened the box on the coffee table and tipped it so Easy could see. Inside was a pinky finger.

"Your pal, Dex. Had to happen, keep the wolves from the door, you know? We have a reputation to uphold."

Easy stared at the dead flesh. He stared at the glass of puke. Unsure which was worse.

"C'mon, kid," said Clown, "take door A. I'm tellin' ya."

"Okay," said Easy.

"Good," said Cimini.

"Good," said Clown. "Now listen up." Then Clown whispered some very interesting things in his ear.

"So what are you waiting for?" asked Mike.

Easy reached for the glass. "One request."

Cimini grinned. "The balls on this kid. Okay, what?"

"Real cool cucumber on the ask," said Clown, "we need this."

Easy took a breath. And go. "After I drink that glass of puke I get to talk with you for two minutes. Alone."

A few minutes later, sucking on like twenty breath mints, Easy stopped talking. He'd done it, emptied the glass. Hands down the worst, most disgusting thing he'd ever done. All the while, Clown whispering into his ear, "Chug, chug, chug." Such a shit disturber. Then, as agreed, Cimini had asked Big Mike and Tiny to go upstairs, though they both, especially Big Mike, went unwillingly.

"You through?" Cimini asked.

"Yes," said Easy.

Cimini mulled this over. "Okay, assuming I believe you, what it is that that you think I should do with this information?" He looked at Easy, a red blush rising to the surface of his cheeks. Still calm but a storm was brewing.

"I just thought you should know."

Cimini nodded. "I see. And now I do." He got up, paced.

Easy sat back, more than a little satisfied. It'd been fun shooting holes through Cimini's life with the ammo Clown had given him, taking aim at everything the man held precious, especially right after he made Easy drink puke. Bang bang, shot you down.

Your wife doesn't go to yoga on Thursday nights.

Your wife is cheating on you.

Your wife is cheating on you with your friend and body-guard, Big Mike.

And your son maybe looks a bit like Big Mike, no?

Cimini stopped pacing. He put a hand on Easy's shoulder. "You don't move, okay? Not a muscle."

"Whatever you say."

When Cimini had left the room, Clown popped out from underneath his shirt collar and ran down Easy's arm, hopping onto the table. He smelled the empty glass. "Gross."

"No shit," said Easy.

"Okay, we don't have long. Go to the liquor cabinet, in the corner, behind the pool table."

"For a drink?"

"Oh my God. You're an even dumber mule than I gave you credit for. No. There's a drawer."

"Okay."

"Well open it, asshole. There's a pistol inside. What the young 'uns used to call a 'Saturday Night Special.' Empty the bullets, put 'em in your pocket. Call it insurance, just in case."

As Easy did so, some things fell into place, made sense.

Clown always said they'd be going to the top together, just never the top of what. "You had me rip off Tiny so I'd get pulled in for a talk. How else would I get close enough to talk with the man himself, right? So this was all about setting me up to be the next Big Mike? There's no way Mr. Cimini keeps him on now."

Clown guffawed. "Kid, you ain't wrong, but you ain't that right either."

Easy sat back down. Clown was doing calisthenics on the table. Torso twists. Deep knee bends. Jumping jacks. "Clown," said Easy. "How do you know what you know? Like about the wife and his son being Big Mike's?"

Clown grinned. "The wife, because I heard them talking earlier today when the old guy was in the can. The kid thing, I don't know if it's true. But did you see the old bastard's face? It's like he felt something was wrong all along."

"But I didn't know that. And…"

Clown stopped his quad stretch. "'And' what?"

"And you're…"

"Go ahead."

"…Me," said Easy, voicing what he'd never said, all these years. The annoying little fucker had been around so long he didn't give it much thought. But, ultimately, he'd always believed Clown was his psyche, his instinct, the devil on his shoulder given what appeared, to him at least, as a physical form.

The fit of laughter bent Clown over. He had to put his hands on his knees and take a few deep breaths to regain control. "Oh, that's priceless. Kid, I love ya, but you really are thicker than a stack of phone books sometimes. You thought I was you all these years?"

"Well, a part of me."

"Like an imaginary friend?"

"I guess."

"Damned if that ain't kinda sweet. Naïve, but sweet."

Upstairs, the basement door opened. Footsteps descended.

"Okay, sshh," said Clown, jumping from the table to the

couch, where Cimini had been sitting prior. "This is the final act in a very long play. Don't fuck this up for us now." Clown disappeared behind the couch cushion.

Cimini appeared at the bottom of the stairs, staggering slightly. Hands, shirt, covered in blood. An open straight razor, blade glistening crimson, dropped to the floor. "Shit, I've seen that movie a thousand times and now I know why Travis cries at the end," he said, blankly.

Easy didn't know who Travis was but moved to stand. There was a large screwdriver sticking out of Cimini's gut. "You okay, Mr. Cimini?"

"Just sit. Let me get a drink."

Easy sat, stared at the wall. He heard the shaky clink of a bottle against a glass. He heard Cimini gulp it down. He heard him pour another. He heard the drawer in the liquor cabinet open and shut. Then, no strength left in his legs, Cimini sat down on the couch and leveled the pistol at Easy with a trembling hand. "You were right," he said. "So I slit his throat. And I made Tiny watch. Said this was how a real man handled his problems."

"Mr. Cimini, where's your wife?"

"Oh, out at the library with the boy. Same time every week. I'm not a monster. Though I did leave a surprise in the kitchen for when they get home. Then we'll have ourselves a little chat about yoga night. Now you, talk. How'd you know? You been following my wife?"

"Uh…" said Easy, as a cowboy climbed out of Cimini's shirt pocket. About the same size as Clown, wearing a cowboy hat and cowboy boots. He leaned forward and whispered into Cimini's ear. Easy closed his eyes and opened them again. Nope. All still happening. And then there was Clown, creeping along the back of the couch. He looked at Easy and shook his head, putting his finger to his lips. When Clown was close enough, he jumped out and tackled the cowboy. The two small figures tumbled down to the floor.

"Well, will you look at that," said Cimini.

Clown and the cowboy fought dirty. Grunts and groans. Rabbit punches, eye gauges, knees to the groin. Playing for keeps. But the cowboy seemed to be tiring and Clown was gaining the upper hand.

Cimini grunted. "So you have one too, huh? Prick's ain't they? I was going to be a fireman before he showed up."

"What do you call him?"

"Wild Bill. You?"

"Clown."

"Original."

"What'd he tell you just now?"

"That I'm bleeding pretty bad, to get to the hospital. But fuck that." He ripped the screwdriver out, wincing. Blood sprayed. "But he's just looking out for himself. I go, he goes." Cimini fixed Easy with a glassy-eyed stare. His lights were dimming. "You know, Easy, you look kind of familiar to me. I couldn't place it but seeing that little clown made me realize. In 1959, I was like you, shaking down pill dealers for their supply. Steal from the criminals, who are they gonna complain to? Had me a partner, name of Roy Baker, who used to be a circus clown. Our families went way back together. Ol' Roy, he was a character. Sneaky, clever and vicious as the day was long. But we got in a little deep one time, made a big score off a connected guy, and his crew tracked us down. We had to run. Only Roy was older than me and had that limp from a circus accident. Something about an elephant going crazy, stampeding in the big top. A bunch of other clowns were killed."

The gun dropped out of Cimini's hand.

Clown had his hands around Wild Bill's throat.

Wild Bill made gurgling sounds.

Cimini continued, saying how he couldn't let them get their hands on Roy, who was too wily to take all the blame. And they were partners, not friends. Too much family drama in their past. "So it was him or me," said Cimini. "And it wasn't going to be me. I killed him and took his share of the loot. And I'll be damned if that clown isn't the spitting image of Roy. And you for that matter. You could be his kin."

So many questions. Only one, the least important, was clear enough to voice. "Who's Travis?" Easy asked.

"The boy in 'Old Yeller.' Had that rabid dog that had to be put down. Stupid, lovable mutt."

It was the last thing Henry Cimini would ever say.

And there were no more gurgling sounds from Wild Bill.

Okay, kid, you deserve to hear more about this, I'll grant you that. So get busy getting those bullets back in the gun and put it back where you found it. Then wipe it down and anything else you may have touched. Big Mike put us in a pretty position, what with stabbing him with that screwdriver. All this looks like now is a disagreement between known scumbags gone wrong. And your hands stay clean. I figured you'd have to shoot the bastard or something. Though first up will be dealing with Tiny, who's probably cowering in the closet in a puddle of his own piss. But there's enough cash hidden in this house to make all that possible, don't you worry about that.

Okay, where to start. I was born in '59, after Cimini shot your great-grandfather in the gut. Born in a pool of blood on motel room carpet for one thing: pure, sweet vengeance. But we can't just go up to anyone and say 'kill that guy over there, he done my host wrong.' Nah, it's family shit, in the DNA. Passed down. Blood feuds. Eye-for-an-eye. Has been since the beginning, will be until the end of time.

So I waited and waited, until your grandfather was old enough to understand. But I was too direct and he had this uptight, do-gooder streak. Knew Roy to be the drunk, deadbeat dad and criminal lowlife he was and thought the past should stay in the past. Same with your dad. I wasn't family enough for him, so he joined the military like a sheep and it killed him. Yeah, you never met him, did you? Right, he knocked your mom up the night before he deployed.

Anyway, I changed my game plan with you, brought you along slow. Kept you in the dark, only let you know what you needed to know. But you did good, kid, believe me. You're special, a lowdown, mean son-of-bitch. Like Roy. But smarter at the same time. And we did it, you and me. We got revenge.

Okay, I get why you're looking at me like that. I've done you dirty, if you look at it a certain way. Leadin' you down a path, so to speak. And yeah, getting you to rip off Tiny all those times could've just got you shot in the head but it was a risk I had to take. I needed an in. Needed to be invited into his home. Cimini stayed real separate from all the street-level stuff the last few years. Played the husband, the businessman.

And Wild Bill did the same thing, believe me. Groomed Cimini and had him kill Roy in '59 for something Roy did in the past. I told you, these blood feuds never die.

Okay, done? Great, let's get the cash and blow this popsicle stand.

Easy found Tiny sitting on the couch in the upstairs living room. He was as pale as the off-white walls but to his credit he hadn't pissed his pants. Easy put the duffel bag on the coffee table. It was full of cash from a safe in the basement, to which Clown conveniently knew the combination. Clever little freak.

"What happened down there?" Tiny asked.

"He bled out," said Easy.

"I saw the whole thing. Mike tried to blame it on you, say you were just spinning lies to get under Cimini's skin, but it was obvious. He's had a hard on for Trina for years. Before I knew it, Cimini had flicked open the blade and slit Mike's throat. But Mike knew something was up and must've grabbed the screwdriver off the side table before they sat down. Managed to stab him a few times. Good riddance, I say. They were both assholes."

Easy threw him a few rolled bundles of cash. "This square us?"

"Sure. You were never here."

"Trina will play along?"

"No doubt. She's smart."

Easy zipped up the duffel bag. "Give her this. If the cops freeze bank accounts and assets, this'll help."

"What about you?"

"Got something else in mind. Maybe you want to assist?"

"Depends."

Easy had a plan. Not Clown's for once. His own. Because, he told Tiny, it'd be chaos for a while with both Cimini and Big Mike gone. "The kind of chaos where it might take an organization a few days to get up and running smooth again."

"Maybe," said Tiny.

"Well, maybe before that happens we visit those stash spots you know about. Take as much as we can. Call it a business loan from your semi-uncle. My pal Dex can move it. He might be short a finger but he's long on contacts. With the boss and two-man gone and his squad starvin' for product, we could build an empire of our own."

"Nice," said Clown, from Easy's shirt pocket. "I would've just taken the cash but you're planning for the future. I can respect that. The ol' 'Don't give a man a fish, teach him how to fish' routine."

"Like you said, Clown, all the way to the top."

Tiny nodded. "Deal. I'm with you, Easy. But one thing: please don't call me a clown, okay?"

The miniature fireman, complete with long coat, boots and hat, sat on the kitchen counter, legs swinging from the custom marble top, and watched while the mother screamed at the 9-1-1 operator and then screamed when the cops arrived and then screamed when the morgue guys carted the bodies away. She screamed real good and loud. Sold it pretty well, considering. Of course she had no idea what had happened or why and simply come back from being out with her son to find her husband's employee dead in the kitchen and her husband dead in the basement and my husband was just a successful businessman, whatever do you mean?

But the fireman, spitting image of a young Henry Cimini, had been born in blood for one thing and one thing only so mostly he watched the boy. The two-year-old was still crapping in his diapers and said words so only the mother could understand, but he looked okay in the brains department. He'd have to work on his shapes, though, he was currently trying to shove a round block into a square hole.

"Psst, kid. Not that one, the blue one."

The kid looked up.

The fireman waved.

The kid smiled, waved back.

COMMAND PERFORMANCE
Warren Moore

"Is there an empty room where I can get ready?" James Pruitt spoke to the woman at the nurses' station on the children's wing. He opened his bag toward her, and showed her his props and makeup. "I'll only need it for about ten minutes."

"Even to get made up? You must be really fast." Pruitt read her ID badge—Jenna S.

"No, not really—we just don't do as much makeup as we used to these days. With the horror movies and stuff like that, too many people get creeped out by the full whiteface. And God knows I'm not here to scare the kids." He shook his head. "Just being here is probably scary enough. So I keep the makeup pretty simple and pretty limited. Same with the costume. Really, it's the attitude, the character, that makes the clowning, anyway." He smiled. "But is there a place I can use?"

The nurse thought a moment, and said, "There's the break room. It has a bathroom with a mirror. Will that work?"

"That'll be great. Can you tell me how to get there?"

"I can do better than that," she said. "Follow me." She led him down a main hallway, then a left and a right. He saw the things he always saw at the hospital: empty gurneys, carts with food trays.

Pruitt walked past a room with the door ajar and saw the

foot of a bed and a tired-looking woman sitting in a chair below a wall-mounted TV. Someone's mom, he thought as Spongebob's cackle drifted out the door. And he heard something else, from his escort, but he hadn't made it out. "Excuse me?"

"I said, 'How long have you been doing this?'"

"Well, when I was in high school, I was at a street fair and they were doing little clown classes for kids. It seemed kind of fun, and it turned out I liked it. So it kind of became a part-time job for me, doing birthday parties and school carnivals, stuff like that. It helped me pay my way through college.

"I even studied it for a while, got a Theater Arts minor. Learning about different characters, the history, different bits. But it was strictly a part-time thing, and after college I settled down, started a family—the things people do."

He didn't have to close his eyes to see it. Linda with her dark hair pulled back into a ponytail and the bluest eyes he'd ever seen, honest to God. And a couple of years after that, little Beth.

"But when our daughter was seven, she woke up one morning and said her head hurt. We kept her home from school, and by three, she asked us to turn the TV on, because it was time for her show. But the TV was on. She just couldn't see it.

"We learned later that the tumor had been there for a while— it had to have been, even though it grew fast. And there just wasn't anything they could do, and three days later..." Pruitt let it trail off. The doctors had told him she hadn't been in pain. That was the only kindness of it. If she had hurt, Pruitt didn't want to think of what he could have done, what he might have thought he had to do.

A lot of things had trailed off, he thought. After the funeral— how could a box that small hold someone who had smiled so big?—there was too much silence in the house. A gray streak formed in Linda's hair, and after a time, the silence in the house grew too big for the house to hold even the two of them, and the divorce seemed like a mere confirmation of something that had happened three days after Beth's headache.

"Oh, God," the nurse said. "I'm so sorry."

"Yeah," Pruitt said. "Me too. But one day I was at the cemetery, you know, and I realized that even if I hadn't been able to do anything for Beth, maybe I could make other people—other kids—happy. And that's how I got back into it, and I've done it for a couple of years. Sometimes knowing I can make people smile, well, it reminds me that I can, too."

They had stopped at the break room by then, and the woman said she'd go back to the station, but that she'd show him to the Day Room when he was ready. Pruitt thanked her, went into the bathroom, and got to work.

He had developed his makeup over the years. The red circles on the cheeks fading into his natural complexion, a more defined red circle at the tip of the nose, black laugh lines at the corners of the eyes, and some white around the mouth, but only enough to set off the lipstick smile. Eyebrows slanting slightly up toward the midline of the face. A few freckles completed the look. Friendly. He slipped on some baggy pants with deep pockets for some of the props, and slipped a sportcoat even Bobby Knight would have found in bad taste (he had found it at Goodwill) over his light blue polo shirt. He messed his hair up, and slapped on a propeller beanie. Show time, or it would be once he got to the Day Room.

As Pruitt retraced his way through the hallway, he passed the door where he had heard Spongebob earlier. The woman was standing by the door, talking to a doctor. Her face was blank and tired, and the doctor's was only slightly more animated. Pruitt stopped and got a drink from a hallway water fountain. You have to be careful once the makeup is on.

He sipped carefully and heard a couple of words, even though they were softly spoken and the fountain was running. Palliative...hospice. As he stood back up, he saw a sticker on the chart the doctor was holding. It was white, with red letters: DNR/DNI. Pruitt was walking away as the doctor slipped the chart into the holder beside the door.

He got back to the nurses' station without any difficulty, and Jenna was waiting for him. "It's so sweet of you to do this," she said.

"It's okay," he said. "When Beth...when we lost Beth, all I wanted to do was give her something that might distract her for a few minutes. I told her stories, but I don't know if she heard them. The TV was running at the end, but, well...I don't know.

"But if I can do this and make it a little better even for just a little bit? Okay. And besides, most of these kids are gonna go home. We might as well give them a show so it might not be scary for their brother or sister, or if they have to come back." And they were at the Day Room door, with a plaque thanking a local business for its generosity. Jenna swiped her ID through a card reader, and the double doors swung open.

His smile was genuine: "I'm Jimbo! What's going on?" There were children ranging in age from toddlers sitting in wagons to a couple of teenagers playing 8-ball, with a number of adults around the edges of the room.

Pruitt was rushed by three or four of the young ones. He'd guess them to be in the kindergarten to third grade range. One little girl wore a floral band around her shaven head. He saw the dots of a tattoo that had been placed there for the radiotherapy. He reached into a pocket of his sportcoat and produced a ridiculous fake flower with eyelashes on it. "Would you care for a flower, miss?"

She eyed him warily. "Does it squirt water when I smell it?"

"Don't be ridiculous! You watch far too much television." He handed her the flower, leaned over to sniff it himself, and pushed a button that had it spray him directly in the forehead. "It squirts water when I smell it." The children laughed as he dabbed his forehead with a handkerchief, and things were rolling along.

Pruitt—Pruitt? He was Jimbo now!—pulled some scarves from another pocket, and began slow-motion juggling. As he'd catch one, he acted as if it weighed hundreds of pounds, and would hoist it merely to flutter back down. After a bit, a little boy asked if he could try. Jimbo said, "We can try, but these things are heavy."

The child took one and said, "This isn't heavy at all!"

"Hm. You must be stronger than you look." And on with the show.

He occasionally saw some of the parents using the cameras on their cell phones as he worked the room, but his focus was on the kids as he worked gags into bits, pulled coins from ears, and blew soap bubbles for some of the smallest ones. Yet another pocket revealed a pump that looked like a Flit gun, and now it was time for balloon critters.

And for half an hour, he hardly thought of Beth at all.

At the end of his act, he accepted hugs from the children, and even some from the occasional mom or dad, and said he hoped to see them all soon—but not there. And he pressed against the crash bar on one of the double doors and stepped out of the room, followed by the sound of applause.

Jenna was standing in the hallway when he finished and slouched against the wall by the door. "That was really great, Mr. Pruitt! I was watching through the window in the door."

"You're very kind. The important thing is that they seemed to enjoy it."

"I'm sure they do it breaks up the routine, but in a good way, you know?"

He nodded, and after a breath, said, "Well, I guess I'd better be getting back home. Do you mind if I use the break room again?"

"No problem—do you remember how to get there?"

"Yeah. Thanks for all your help." He flipped her a half-wave, half-salute, and headed back down the hall, glancing over his shoulder to watch as Jenna returned to her station.

When he passed what he thought of as the Spongebob Room— he knew it had a number, but he hadn't noticed it earlier—the door was ajar, but he didn't hear the television. He couldn't resist; glancing both ways, he then stepped into the room.

A little boy lay in the bed. From his size, Pruitt guessed the child might be eight or nine. But his eyes were impossibly, immeasurably old and distant. "Hello," Pruitt said. "I'm Jimbo."

The child spoke softly; Pruitt had to strain to hear him over the sounds of the machinery, the devices keeping the boy alive. "I'm Keith. Are you real?"

"Yeah."

"Okay. I'm not sure sometimes. Sometimes the medicine makes me see things."

"Where's your mom?"

"She's gone to fix supper for my brother. She'll bring me back something tonight, too, but I don't really want it."

"Would you like me to turn the TV on for you?"

"No. I've seen all the shows before. I'm just tired."

"Okay. I'll go, but I was walking by your room earlier, and I wanted to say hi."

"I don't get many visitors. They won't let the kids from school visit me, and when grownups come by, they don't really know what to say." Keith paused. "I'm not going to get better. I'm going to die."

Pruitt almost lapsed into the automatic things one says, the "Don't be silly" and "You don't know that's, but he looked at Keith's eyes again, and thought about the sticker on the chart, and so he didn't say those things. Instead, he said, "I had a daughter. Her name was Beth."

"Did she die?" Pruitt nodded. "Did it take a long time?"

"No. She got sick, and then she was gone in a few days."

"Were you there?"

"Yes." And I never left, he thought. I'm still there.

"I don't think I want my mom to be here." The ghost of a smile flickered across his face. "I don't think I want to be here. I mean, now. I've been here a really long time."

"I'm sorry, Keith. I wish you didn't have to be."

"Something I don't get."

"Yeah?"

"People tell me that when I die—" the words sounded matter of fact, like "if it rains," "—When I die, I'm gonna be with Jesus, and I won't hurt any more, and all sorts of cool stuff."

"A lot of people think that," Pruitt said.

"Do you think that?"

"I don't know, Keith. I hope so. I hope so for Beth, and for you, and well, for me sooner or later."

And then Pruitt say the anger in the boy's old, old eyes. "Then why are they making me stay here?"

"Your family would miss you."

"They will anyway. And I'm tired." He inhaled again. "Did your daughter hurt when she died?"

"Maybe at first—that's how we learned she was sick. But at the end? I don't think so."

The boy nodded. "Can you do that for me?" Pruitt took an involuntary step back, bumping the back of his head on the TV mount.

"I can't do that—look at me! I'm a clown. I want to make people smile, and laugh, and be happy."

"Then make me happy," the boy said. "Tell me a joke."

"What did one snowman say to the other snowman?"

"I give up."

"Do you smell carrots?"

It took a second, but Keith smiled, and made a stuttering noise that Pruitt thought might be a laugh. And then he said, "You made me smile. Now can you make me not hurt anymore?"

And if you asked him later, James Pruitt would say it was like he was watching someone else as he picked up a pillow and held it down for a short time, and slipped out the door again and finished his trip to the break room. Indeed, he realized that he hardly had to hold the pillow—its own weight was probably enough, once the oxygen tube slipped out. He heard an alarm after a few minutes, but didn't hear the running feet that he had heard when Beth's alarm went off.

***

Back in his street clothes, Pruitt made his way toward the exit, passing the nurse's station once more. Jenna was there, and he saw her eyes were slightly red. He asked if she was okay.

"You think you'd get used to it—losing them. That's what happens here. But sometimes it's still hard."

Pruitt nodded. "It is. But you do what you can. You try to help them, in whatever way you can."

"I know you get it," she said. "You've been through it. And now you do this."

He nodded. "You try to make them as happy as you can."

FOOL HARDY
Patricia Abbott

I don't occupy a spot in the Clown's Corridor myself, but I have painted many of the faces on display there. Once I saw the fruit of Howard Tibbal's life work—an exact three-quarter-inch-to-the-foot scale replica of Ringling Bros. and Barnum & Bailey Circus, housed in Sarasota, I was fascinated by the thought of painting miniatures. As charming as it is though, Tibbal's work wasn't exactly what I had in mind. I wasn't interested in fashioning miniature folding chairs, elephant poop, tiny tubs of buttery popcorn or cones of neon cotton candy. It was the faces that fascinated me—the grease-painted ones. Clowns became my passion. But they were also the subject of more than one nightmare over the years. I wonder how often passion is mingled with fear.

My goal, and that of my eventual employer, Mr. P was to capture the pusses of practicing clowns for his project, the Clown's Corridor. Mr. P purchased a deserted warehouse on Pattison Avenue in south Philadelphia and housed the collection there. He filled it with as much reasonably priced clown memorabilia as he could lay his hands on. There is a wide-ranging assortment of artifacts to be had if you hunt around. Clowns have a devoted following and collecting the accessories and paraphernalia of their work seems to be part of the interest.

What circus poster doesn't feature a clown in a prominent role? Can you remember a Halloween night when a clown didn't show up? And tell me that clown on your porch wasn't as frightening as the vampire or a witch. What other Stephen King book holds half the terror of *It*?

But the most important component of Mr. P's collection, for me at least, were the faces of the clowns, each one a copyright or patent of sorts. We followed the example of the British and began to semi-legitimize the legal standing of each face, assigning a number and creating a paper facsimile. Professional credentials were required, of course. A clown for hire at children's' birthday parties didn't qualify. Nor did a clown who did a yearly stint in a parade. Over time, our rules solidified into something specific: the clown must derive an income from the profession, his career must exceed a certain number of years, he/she must be a member of a professional organization, he/she must have created a distinctive face. The last rule was really the primary point of the Corridor: to capture those faces.

At first, I painted each face and a stub of a torso on a small three-inch by four-inch canvass. But in the end, we followed the British tradition and used porcelain eggs. Making the faces three-dimensional made all the difference: it brought them to life. This practice began in '46 when Stan Bult painted many of the faces of his time. The custom has continued on and off in England over the years. Various artists have picked up the baton, and although each artist has his or her own style, the parade of distinct faces, but with certain similarities, makes it a seamless collection.

If I had to critique my own work, I'd say I tend to paint a more benign face than a clown might intend. Oh, the clown is recognizable but perhaps a bit less threatening. Working alone as I often do, I shied away from a face likely to haunt me in my dreams. Once or twice, I have been forced to do a face over because of an overly pleasant demeanor. But generally I'm able to instill a bit more tenderness than the clown intended. Who wants a Dorian Grey in the Corridor after all?

I am proud of the role I've played in the Clown Corridor, but here is my beef. My work has consistently been undervalued. Each egg takes several days to paint and yet my salary for each one is a mere hundred dollars. Mr. P assumes I create the eggs for the love of it rather than as an income. He's mistaken. Both figure equally. Every six months or so, I appear in his office and make my case for a raise. I'm not greedy. I didn't expect to become rich from my labors. A new clown only comes along every so often after all, and the fees never amount to much over the course of a year. But Mr. P is parsimonious, insisting he hardly makes ends meet.

"Do I look like a rich man, Alfred," he said the last time I complained, showing me the tattered hems of his trousers.

But I watched the fans line up when the Clown Corridor opened at ten o'clock six days a week and saw that at fifteen dollars a head, money was being made. Perhaps not a fortune but enough. And despite his many costumes, posters, photographs, videotapes, and other artifacts, it was the Corridor of Eggs that attracted the biggest crowds. And it was my artistry that sold those tickets. A visitor risked being crushed in the narrow passage on a rainy Saturday. So over time, I became more and more aggrieved at my situation and determined to find a solution. An occasional shouting match never cleared the air, and I was considering handing in my notice when a clown by the name of Fool Hardy entered the picture.

The face Fool Hardy created for himself was not one of the more remarkable ones, but was unique due to the multi-colored freckles painted on it. It must have taken him, or an assistant, an hour to get them exactly right. I assumed before I painted his egg that he used stick-on freckles, but no, he painted each one of the twenty-four himself. His face was finished off with dark blue lips, dominant, almost threatening, eyebrows, and spiky neon green hair. According to the records, I first painted his egg in 2000.

Fool Hardy, like a number of other clowns, asked me to paint a second egg to keep for himself. For this I was paid two hundred and fifty dollars, a fairer price, but still not enough to give up my day job teaching art classes to arthritic seniors at the Community College of Philadelphia. There is something sad about not earning a living from an endeavor you've poured your soul into. I realize there are far greater artists who share my failure, but it doesn't make it much easier.

One day not long ago, I came home to find Fool Hardy on my doorstep. Having only seen him in his clown regalia, the street clothes made him difficult to identify. I backed away from the light, trying futilely to recall his name.

I was easy for him to find. I hadn't seen any reason to keep my address a secret and, in fact, I often painted the eggs at home where I had everything I needed. Although I used photographs for most of the work, seeing the clown helped make the eggs more memorable. It was in the movements, the facial expressions, the voice, that I got to know my subjects.

Fool Hardy didn't say a word until the door was closed. When he was satisfied we were alone, he flopped into my favorite chair and began to talk. Like most of the clowns I'd known, his feet moved perpetually as if the big shoes were still on them and his gestures and facial expressions were demonstrative. The back rows could be very far away under the big top, and circus crowds did not tote opera glasses.

"You'd be surprised at how many circuses no longer hire clowns, Albert," he began.

"Alfred, I corrected him.

"Alfred. Yes, well, Cirque du Soleil has pushed traditional circus acts off the stage, priming the audiences to demand smoke and mirror effects." He paused to blow his nose. "So a clown like me has to find other ways to make a living. Have any Kleenex?" he asked, tossing his used one on the coffee table.

"Our stories are not so different," I told him, nodding toward a box of tissues and thinking it had been six months since I had painted a new egg.

"So anyway," he said, ignoring my remark as I knew he would, "I had to find a way to supplement my income when the circus I worked for, Artie's Party, cut my hours. Twice."

I have to admit my curiosity as to how any of this concerned me was growing.

"Stupidly, I decided to rob a party store. I'd done it once or twice so it wasn't foreign territory." He paused to swipe his dripping nose. "I felt more in control in a costume so I wore mine." He giggled. "Just like my name, right? Fool."

"You dressed like Fool Hardy for the job?" The guy was not a widely known clown but still...

He nodded, then shrugged. "It put me at ease. A clown feels most like himself in his costume. I chose a store where the camera was out of commission. Big crack right down the middle of the screen. Like the last guy robbing the place tossed a brick at it. So there'd only be the clerk's memory to pin it on me. I thought I'd just be some anonymous clown to him, especially since I omitted the freckles. With all the clown antics going on lately I figured he'd be scared shitless."

"And?" I said.

"He's got this big smile as soon as I came in the door. Turns out he watched me on TV as a kid. On some dopey show I did. Couldn't remember my name though. Nor the name of the show. Kept calling me Smarty Pants. I was relieved to hear him get it wrong. So I robbed the place anyway. Shocked the pants off him. That his childhood hero was a thief. Seemed like the only thing to do." He paused. "I am betting those freckles didn't stand out so much on black and white TVs, which was what this guy had, believe it or not."

Smarty Pants was in the clown corridor all right. But had a completely different look. Odd that the clerk had mixed up the two.

"So anyway, the cops are likely to march the clerk over to the Corridor eventually, Alfred. Maybe even today. Get him to pick me out that way instead of from a lineup or a sketch."

"Sorry, I don't remember what you said. When did I paint you?"

"Around 2000," Fool Hardy said. "About when I had that gig on the kid's TV show. I was riding high then. Mr. Papadopolos called one day, asking me to pose for my egg. It was some other guy doing them then, I think." He squinted at me.

"No, it was me. Me, with a lot more hair on my head." I looked down. "Less belly too."

"I guess. Well anyway, that wouldn't happen today. My getting in the Corridor, I mean. Doubt I could get approved."

"Well, once you're in, you stay." I paused. "Even after death."

"I want that egg out of there now. That guy's gonna finger me before the day's out."

I started shaking my head. "Mr. P's got lists and cross lists. If your head is missing, he'll know it."

"But what if it wasn't missing by the next time he waltzed in? What if Fool Hardy was a female clown with large breasts and a neon green wig—but just for a few hours. Or a clown that's half dog and half cat. What if that clerk couldn't find a clown that looked anything like the one he saw?"

I could tell he'd given this some thought, but I shook my head harder, still not getting it. "You'll never get away with it. Mr. P knows his clowns."

"We don't have to fool Mr. P. Just this party store doofus. Once he can't ID me in there, life will go on. You can return my egg after the guy leaves. Look, I only got six hundred bucks in that robbery. How hard will they look for a petty criminal?" He stood up. "I'll split the take with you if you substitute a female clown with a neon wig. Or whatever you like. Fool Hardy becomes a dame for one afternoon."

"I'd have to paint it too quickly." I'd never spent less than eight hours on a head. "Plus I'm taking risks."

"Okay, I'll give you all of the dough. The whole enchilada.

Six hundred bucks for your time and trouble. It doesn't have to be your finest work. Just good enough not to stand out." He stood and removed his wallet, began thumbing through bills. "Just my luck this one guy in a million remembers me from the nineties." He paused. "Kind of flattering though."

I spend the next two hours creating a female face. It was kind of fun, inventing a clown of my own. Her face was catlike-sort of like Michelle Pfeiffer in that Batman movie. It was scary and sexy at the same time. Luscious red lips, lots of shiny black.

"Pretty good," he said approvingly via cell after I texted him the photo. "Can you slip it in there pronto?"

I nodded. Michelle Pfeiffer, or Michelle from Hell as I began to think of her, took the place of Fool Hardy.

When the cop and the store clerk trooped in later that day, they were stymied. No egg resembled the clown who'd robbed the store, and escorted by one of Mr. P's minions, they soon left the premises. I put the real Fool Hardy egg back fifteen minutes later and stuck Michelle from Hell in my pocket. It was unlikely any Philadelphia cop would invest further time in a minor crime with no victim.

I had spent little time in the Corridor for years so I figured I'd take a quick look. The place was impressive. I had to read the placards to identify most of the occupants, but there was Rudy, the Rascal, a clown I had struggled with for weeks. And Petunia Pickpocket, a sweet-faced rapscallion who appeared on a noontime kid's show in the sixties. Clowns that were actually played by children were rare, and Petunia was played by a dwarf, in fact. I picked the egg up to admire the craft of an artist from long before my time. The paint he used was fading, and I wondered if I should try and touch it up. Maybe I should look them all over. Mr. P might pay me for some restorations.

There must have been a timer on the lighting system in the Corridor because as I held Petunia in my hands, the lights dimmed to near darkness. I was startled enough to drop the egg and it broke at my feet. No more Petunia Pickpocket. Of course,

I could easily recreate her from the sketches. Should I pull the card identifying her and move the other eggs closer to bridge the gap until I made a copy? As I began to rearrange the eggs, I realized too late that the removal of one egg set into motion a domino effect. It started slowly as I watched in horror. But suddenly, the eggs began to move faster, rolling down, helter-skelter, and falling off the long tables one by one, in a sort of Humpty Dumpty fashion. I tried to catch them as they reached the table's end, but they rolled erratically as eggs do, some bouncing off the table's edges before they even reached me. I looked in vain for a basket or hat to catch them. Nothing handy. I threw myself on top of the ones nearing the edge.

When the maelstrom ended, when I finally managed to find the light switch and the room was fully lit, I counted at least a dozen eggs completely destroyed. Another dozen or more were chipped or the paint blemished. I began to gather them up but then decided to let them lay where they fell. There was no good way out of this mess. The large number of missing eggs would be noticed immediately. I looked around. Could I create a feasible explanation for what happened here? Perhaps I could make it look as if the place had been robbed and eggs were a casualty of the reckless thieves? Perhaps the door was left open when the cop and clerk left, the minion shirking his duties. Better yet would be another point of entry since Mr. P's guards were so diligent. I spotted a skylight at the end of the middle hallway and grabbing a broom from the janitor's closet and standing on a stool, smashed it.

Quickly, making my face up to look as much as possible like the Michelle Pfeifer egg so no one could ID me, I tiptoed out, using my handy broom to destroy what seemed like the sole camera. It occurred to me that Fool Hardy's theft had relied on a broken camera and my escape, if it was that, would too. I spent the night tossing and turning, trying to concoct a story that covered me.

The phone rang before nine. "Alfred," Mr. P said, "something strange went on down here last night. I let some cop in and he must have left the door open when he left. Someone—kids I'm betting—got inside and had themselves a party. Broke a lot of the eggs. Must have knocked themselves out laughing. Probably high on coke."

"That's horrible," I said, relieved he'd settled on this scenario without any prompting. "Can I help you clean up?"

"Naw, I got my guys on that. Look, I need you to make new eggs. As fast as you can. I took out some insurance on the place so I can pay you better than usual. What would be a fair price?"

"Five hundred an egg." It didn't take me a second to come up with that figure because I had thought all night about it.

I expected him to balk at such a hefty increase and was ready to settle at three-fifty. But he agreed quickly, which, of course, made me think I had asked for too little. But still.... should I have felt some guilt for being the one who destroyed the eggs? Felt sorry for the loss of other artists' work. But the years of being exploited hardened me.

A few days later, I began to work on the eggs: nineteen in all. I'm proud of the new eggs. I did one more than I broke. I could hardly part with my greatest egg. Michelle from Hell quickly became a fan favorite though no one remembered ever seeing her perform in the flesh. But she had that one performance and I have the selfie to prove it. Darn right.

PAYASOS ASESINOS
Scotch Rutherford

The ominous harbinger of Izzy Stradlin's opening guitar riff choked under the weight of Slash's power chords that crushed like impending doom, matching the opening verse of Guns N' Roses' "My Michelle."

Celina wondered how Axl Rose could have written about her own personal history. Six years before her mom had gotten knocked up by a one of a handful of strangers, on a dirty couch somewhere in an abandoned meat packing plant on the south side of Tarzana. The duct tape around her mouth made her cheeks hot and her palms sweat. Her hands were zip tied behind her back and her palms were clammy. Her ass and her feet were cold, and she couldn't feel anything below the ankles, where they'd wound the zip tie too tight. Mostly the two freaks in the front seat facing forward. Every now and then the one on the passenger side would turn, and flash his freakshow face back in her direction. Their faces were painted up in some demonic looking black and white kabuki face paint that made them look like a cross between ICP and King Diamond. When they'd first grabbed her inside her apartment, they'd come off more like the latter.

Kicking and screaming with her mouth covered, she'd pissed herself, long before they tossed her in the back seat. There was something elemental about faces in black and white greasepaint. Something terrifying. At least there was, until they started to open their mouths, and she realized they were just a couple of clowns.

"I told you to leave it," the one on the right side said.

"Bro, this fuckin' hair metal shit is killing me," the driver said. He sounded like a white boy, and when he finger fucked the dial over to a gangsta rap pop station, she knew he had to be.

The guy on the passenger side was Latino. An Eastsider. She could hear it when he talked. He had to be. He should have known better.

"Whatever. Shut the fuck up. Stop talking so much. Home-girl's right back there," said the passenger side guy.

"Bro, she's probably illegal. She was yapping in Spanish just before we snatched her up. Bitch probably doesn't even speak a lick of English. We got nothing to worry about," the whiteboy said.

They'd grabbed her just as she ended a call to her boyfriend. He was involved. Eighteenth Street, and if he got a hold of these two jabronis, he'd cut off their little dicks and put them in each other's mouths. That was a comforting thought. Too bad her pinche fucking cell phone had rolled under the bed, when these two faggot payasos took her.

Just shut up, okay?" The passenger side guy said. "Just fucking drive."

"Yo, hold up." The whiteboy said, eye fucking the rearview mirror. "How long has that car back there been following us?"

"What car?"

By the time they finally stopped she had no idea how long they'd been driving. It felt like four hours, but when your arms are tied behind your back, your ankles bound, and all your weight pushing on your left shoulder, ten fucking minutes can seem like an eternity. At least she didn't have to pee.

The back door swung open, and the two payasos stood in the doorway, and Celina stared back at them. They were both dressed head to toe in funeral black. One of them, the whiteboy who'd been driving held up a movie camera, and smiled at her like Jack Nicholson as the Joker, before he hissed a snarling snicker. The other one just looked like a sad-faced clown. When the sad-faced clown cut the zip tie around her ankles she kicked him right in his fucking face.

"Fucking puta," the sad-faced clown said, as he lunged into the backseat, and grabbed her by the wrists. As he ripped her out of the backseat, she tried to shriek, but it was no use. Her mouth was covered in duct tape, and he was much stronger. When she was out of the backseat, she could see they were out in the middle of nowhere. A lone 1960s Chevy pickup rolled past. One like her Tio used to drive. She followed it with her eyes, watched it roll past in a cloud of dust as if she wasn't even there, and her heart sank. They'd brought her somewhere out in the desert. East bum fuck. The sun was bleeding into the horizon, and her heart started to race, as they walked her farther and farther from where the car was parked, on the side of a one lane highway. The sad-faced clown held her by the wrists from behind, as he shoved her forward, while the whiteboy clown filmed it. Her nipples were hard because it was cold as fuck, and it was noticeable. Just what she needed. They probably loved that shit.

"This is far enough," the whiteboy said from behind the camera. "Get on your knees."

The sad-faced clown pushed Celina down onto her knees, and the jagged desert ground into her flesh, through thin leggings. The sad-faced clown reached around her and squeezed her tits. "Hell yeah. She's all ready to go. That's what I'm talking about."

Celina wanted to spit right in the dirty fucker's face. The whiteboy cameraman roared with laughter.

"She don't think you're man enough, bro," said the cameraman. "She thinks you're a fuckin' maricon." He let out an obnoxious laugh like a machine gun.

The sad-faced clown took out his dick. Celina recoiled in horror. It was hard and veiny, when he rubbed it against her cheek. She clenched her eyes shut. She felt her throat start to close up, and her breathing became shallow. The two men laughed. The sad-faced clown ripped the duct tape off Celina's mouth. Her lips and mouth were on fire, and she shrieked. The sad-faced clown prodded at her lips with his man wood, but she kept her jaw locked shut.

"So what's up? C'mon, baby," the sad faced clown said. "Kiss it."

Celina knew in that moment, what they were going to do. They were going to film each other with her. One would hold the camera, while he stroked himself, and the other would...she could survive it. She could get through it. As long as they didn't put it in her...her mind flashed back to when she'd come home from school. Her mother was still working long hours at the hospital. She was left in the care of her father and her uncle. When they first did those things to her it felt good. Then it didn't. Then, whenever they did those things to her, she'd always act more and more afraid. It was as if the sooner they saw her terrified, the sooner they would stop. She'd close her eyes. Drown out the heavy breathing and the grunting, and let her mind drift to some animated place, with wide-eyed faces drawn smoothly, as though she were lost in some anime realm on DMT. By the time Celina reached high school, she'd lost her mother to a heroin overdose. That was when she first met her boyfriend, an intense nineteen-year-old, who called himself Little Snoopy. He was hot, and also involved. And that fool loved to put in work. Reality came swift for her uncle, and her old man.

"Yo, that's enough, motherfucker."

Celina's eyes snapped open. She stared in the direction of the voice, into the glowing red dot, next to the lens of the whiteboy's camera. The sad faced clown had put his prick away.

"The time is now motherfuckers," the whiteboy said, as

though to an audience. "Do it."

Celina's heart was already pounding, when the sad-faced clown produced the gun. It was a big silver one, like the ones Samuel L. Jackson and John Travolta had in *Pulp Fiction.*

The sad-faced clown slid the barrel against the side of her head. Celina didn't have to worry about looking terrified. She was shaking so violently she started convulsing. Her eyes snapped shut again.

"Put it in her fuckin' mouth," she heard the whiteboy say. "C'mon, do it."

She felt him press the barrel against her lips, pushing it in against her clenched teeth.

"Suck it, you little whore," the whiteboy shouted, cackling. "Make her fucking suck it!"

Then everything stopped.

"I can't," the sad-faced clown said.

Celina's eyes snapped back open.

"You fucking—" The red light on the camera went out, and then the camera slid off of the whiteboy clown's face. The sun had now disappeared behind him, and his ominous greasepaint covered face dripped with a terrifying resolve.

"Don't get all fuckin' religious on me, bro," the whiteboy said. "We need this. Don't fucking puss out on me. You need this as badly as I do."

"Yeah, but Gabe—"

"What the fuck is wrong with you?"

"It's just that…I don't feel good about this shit. And—"

"Don't you fuckin' trust me?! Look, let's just get this, and get the fuck out of here," the whiteboy said, sounding like a spoiled child. "We've got a fuckin' load to pick up. Now come the fuck on, and stop being a bitch."

Celina watched from the corner of her eye, as the sad-faced clown's mug iced over, then he shoved the barrel against her lips. The camera was back in her face, with the read eye beaming, when the sad-faced clown said, "Open your fucking mouth.

Open your fucking mouth, bitch!" The sad faced clown ripped back Celina's head by her hair, and wedged the barrel into her mouth.

By now she'd lost control of her bowels, and was desperately trying to scream, as the sad-faced clown tried to deep throat her with the metal barrel. Her eyes widened as her heart rate increased. She felt him cock the hammer back.

"Say goodnight, puta."

Celina heard a loud crack, one that seemed to echo. There was a high-pitched ringing in her ears, and then she felt like a giant fist was squeezing first her throat, and then chest, and then her entire body. She couldn't hear anything. Then everything went black. Then there was nothing.

"What the fuck did you do?" Gabe said, dropping the camera.

They both stood over the girl, Luis's right hand shook, still gripping the .45. The girl was lying there motionless. Both men were frozen. Luis studied her face. She seemed to have a look of peace—

"Fucking feel her pulse. What the fuck?" Gabe spat.

Luis dropped the gun, and knelt down next to the body, placing his two fingers on the girl's throat, the way he'd seen them do it on *Law & Order*.

"There's no fucking blood." Gabe said. "It's a fucking starter pistol. That was a blank! The fucking barrel's capped. What the fuck happened?"

Luis's fingers fished around the girl's neck. He couldn't find her pulse, but figured he probably wasn't doing it right. That's when his fingers rubbed against a chain the girl had around her neck. What the fuck, he thought, maybe it's worth something. He pulled the chain up over the girl's shirt, and recognized the Medic Alert symbol on the end of the chain. It looked like the one his cousin Arturo wore on his wrist because he was allergic to shellfish. He turned it over. "What does History of Acute

Myocardial Infarction mean?"

"It means this bitch had a heart attack," Gabe said. "Fuck!"

"Okay, so what the fuck now? Should we just leave her here, under some brush or some shit?" Luis was trying to be rational, and resisted the urge to cross himself.

"Fuck. Fuck. Fuck. Let me think. Shit. No. No way. This might be the sticks, but believe it or not, people come through here. They fly over here. They off-road around here."

"Ah shit. That's right. You from here. Out in the country and shit. This your 'hood."

"No, but close enough," Gabe said. "We can't leave her."

"So what then?"

"We got to bury her."

"Shit," Luis said. "It's fucking cold as shit. Fool, we ain't got no shovel. Plus we got to meet Lassiter by ten. There's no re-scheduling."

"We're going to have to go into town, and find someone with a shovel," Gabe said. "Let's get her up. Help me load her into the trunk."

It was already dark, when they passed a sign that read *Welcome to Searchlight, Nevada*. Luis couldn't help but feel like the terrain looked like the establishing shot for a horror film. "Where the fuck we gonna find a shovel? There ain't shit around here."

The whole thing was supposed to be easy. The whole Creepy Clown fucking thing had spiked, and he and Luis had swooped in, to dominate the whole muthafuckin' urban legend landscape, uploading video after video of clown terrorism, using revolving overseas IP addresses. The Killer Clowns had amassed 996K hits. This mock assassination would've put them over a million hits—with monetization, that put them halfway to the budget they needed for their USC School of Film and Television under-grad thesis film. It was all perfect. All theater, all entertainment. All bullshit, until Luis decided to grab some taco cunt from the projects with a weak fucking heart. But that was okay. It was all part of some divine plan.

"I think I know where we can find a shovel."

A harsh wind rocked the side of the car like turbulence. Finding a Walmart or a hardware store open past dark in Searchlight wasn't likely. From the side of the highway, Wayne's Tavern looked like a beacon against a sea of black desert. It had only been about thirty minutes of searching, but it felt like midnight when they pulled into the lot off 95. The lot was dark and uneven. At the far end there was a big rig parked with no trailer. Under the light of the sign, was a trifecta of pickups. An old Ford, an old Chevy—one with a giant Snap-on Tools rig in the bed, along with some other tools, and one late model Dodge.

Gabe parked the car in the dark corner of the lot, next to the old Chevy. He pulled out two blue packets from underneath the seat. He handed one to Luis, which read *makeup remover* on the side of the packet.

"Get it all off." Gabe said. "This ain't L.A. You feel me? Any of these cats here think we're wearing makeup at all, we're fucked."

Luis was happy to lay into the greasepaint with the alcohol wipes. This gig was up. He just needed to survive the next few hours. There was thirty K worth of glass under the spare tire kit, a dead girl in the trunk. They were due in Vegas in three hours, and still had an hour's worth of driving to do.

They crept up to the old Chevy. Sure enough, some hick fuck had shovels, hoes, and whole gang of tools.

"Shit," Gabe said, when he saw they were padlocked to a tool frame. "Motherfuckin' lockdown."

"Maybe we can bribe this fool with some green," Luis said.

"Hell yeah," Gabe said.

"Now when we get in there, just follow my lead, okay?" Gabe said. "I know how to deal with these fuckin' hicks, you know what I'm saying?"

As they walked up to the entrance of Wayne's Tavern, Luis took out his phone to check the time. That's when he realized he still had the girl's phone. He'd swiped that shit right off the floor, from under the bed in the girl's apartment, thinking it might be worth something. Before he got inside the doorway, he wiped the phone down, and hurled is as far as he could throw. Walking in, Luis followed directly behind Gabe. They were dressed in black hooded sweatshirts and black jeans. There was no way they were going to pass themselves off as locals. Three men in the back, wearing cowboy hats stood around menacingly, holding their pool cues at the ready, while some other redneck was lining up his shot. Some twangy country leaked from a jukebox. For sure that's what it was, but it didn't sound like no Taylor Swift shit. Luis rubbed his neck. There was still some greasepaint he missed. Fuck. He hoped the lynch mob in the back wouldn't notice. Times like these, he was glad he was light skinned.

The bar was a dive alright, with bad lighting and video poker on the bar top. The bartender was a real catch. Remarkably preserved for these parts. Young, maybe twenty-two, with perfect tits, and they looked natural too. The kind a lot of girls back in L.A. paid a fortune for. She met Gabe's eyes with her chin down. Girl had the kind of DSLs any man wood would love to corrupt.

"What can I get you?"

"Whiskey," Gabe said, and held up two fingers.

The bartender poured two shots on the edge of the bar, letting Gabe get a good look down her shirt.

"You fellas on your way to Vegas?"

Gabe turned to his right and saw a fossil of a man at the end of the bar, with his arms folded over the orange glow of a corner one dollar poker machine.

"Yeah," Gabe said offering a snicker. "What gave us away?"

"A look of hope," the old man said. "Folks going the other

way ain't got that."

"What are you drinkin'?" Gabe asked.

"Whiskey," the old man said, holding up his glass, cracking a grin.

The old man was seated to the right of Luis, and Luis could see there was a janitor size wad of keys in front of him, with a Chevy symbol on the key ring.

The bartender placed the two shots in front of Gabe and Luis.

"Here's to hope," Gabe said, raising his shot, and Luis did the same before they both hammered down the shots frat boy style.

The old man sipped his shot of whiskey. "Ya'll a couple o' faggots?"

"Excuse me?" Gabe said, his eyes burning a hole in the old man's forehead.

"Faggots. I just asked if y'all fuck each other in the ass."

The bartender grinned, cocking an eyebrow, while she was wiping down a glass, but said nothing.

"It's fine if y'are. Just, you know. I just can't deal with no faggots."

Gabe gave the old man a firm stare. "We're not gay—"

"Whatever you want to call it—" the old man began.

"No. Nothing like that," Gabe said, cutting him off.

"Nothing like that," Luis added.

"Reason I ask is 'cause the señor here has black makeup on his neck, and both y'all smell like the dime store perfume counter at Woolworth's in Bullhead City. Ya'll smell like a woman."

Gabe and Luis froze.

"So, I just figured ya'll were in some kind of situation."

"Listen, old man, we don't want any trouble," Gabe said. "We're just stopped in here for a quick drink." Gabe pulled out a twenty, and threw it on the bar top.

"Ya'll got a problem?"

Luis sat there static, waiting on the old man.

Gabe tugged on his sleeve. "C'mon, let's go."

"Well, it's too bad ya'll are in such a hurry," the old man said. "I might be able to give you boys a hand. If you're in a fix."

Luis met the old man's stare. "You drive that old Chevy with all them tools sitting in the bed?"

"That's right. Name's Cecil."

Gabe plunked another twenty on the bar top, and eyeballed the old man, tipping his head toward the front door, motioning for the old man to follow.

"So let me get this straight," Cecil said. "Ya'll hit a stray dog? And ya'll want to bury that sunuvabitch in the desert?"

They were standing behind Cecil's old school Chevy.

"It's the right thing to do," Gabe said.

"We'd like to rent a shovel." Luis said. "Fifty bucks."

"Or we'll just buy it off you, Gabe said. "A hundred."

Cecil cocked an eyebrow. "For a dog? Was this pooch wearin' a collar?"

"It's his dog." Luis blurted out.

Gabe shot Luis a look that said, what the fuck are you doing?

"You hit your own dog? Now ya'll ain't makin' no sense," Cecil said.

Luis shot Gabe a look, tipping his head to the right, that said, we better get going.

"I think ya'll better let me get a good look at this pooch," Cecil said.

"No. No, it's ugly," Gabe said. "We can't."

"Now c'mon, boys, I can handle whatever you got back there. I used to put down horses. C'mon, pop the trunk. Let's see her."

Luis had the kind of terrified look, Gabe could see the old man reading. "Three hundred. For the shovel."

"Goddamn. Ya'll really are serious about burying that dog," Cecil said. "Got yourselves a deal."

Gabe reached into his pocket and peeled off three Benjamins from a wad of bills held by a chrome money clip. Cecil unlocked the tool rack, and handed Gabe a big rusty wooden handled flathead shovel from the bed of his truck.

"Better I get your loot then them one-armed bandits," Cecil said, with a chuckle.

Gabe offered up a nervous laugh. Luis just froze.

"I still think ya'll better let me have a look," Cecil said. "I mean for three hundred dollars—"

"No, no. Hey, it's fine. We'll take care of it. In fact, here's a little something extra," Gabe said, pulling off a fourth hundred-dollar-bill and holding it out to Cecil. "For your trouble."

Cecil stared at Benjamin Franklin's face. "Nah, that's alright. You boys have a good night. I can't take any more of your money," Cecil said and headed back into the bar.

"Jesus fucking Christ," Luis hissed. "I thought we were—"

"Especially since ya'll ain't gonna break ground past six inches," Cecil said.

Both Gabe and Luis spun around to see Cecil standing in the doorway of Wayne's Tavern.

"Ground's frozen, boys. It's January for Christ's sake," Cecil said with a snicker. "'Course if ya'll got a body you want to get rid of, I've got me a makeshift crematorium, back at the ranch. But that'll cost you a lot more than three hundred dollars."

Searchlight's higher elevation for the Mojave. It gets a whole lot colder out here than what you're used to. Follow me closely, and don't get lost. This ain't Los Angeleees, Cecil had told them.

"How the fuck did that old man know we were from L.A., anyhow?" Gabe said.

"Probably that big ass USC Trojans bumper sticker you got pasted next to the license plate, fool," Luis said.

It had gotten colder, and the roads had gotten worse since they'd gotten off 95. They followed the old Chevy up a private road, with no sign, up a steep ass hill, that reminded Luis of his cousin's place in Lincoln Heights. Wasn't shit else around when they pulled up to the place. It looked like a big shack from some cowboy movie. Luis figured if shit went south, they could take the old man. Wouldn't nobody find that fool for weeks.

Gabe parked at the top of the dirt road, and shut off the engine. They waited for Cecil to get out of his truck and walk up to the window. Luis pulled the starter pistol from the glove box and wedged it into his waistband, at the small of his back, just before Cecil walked up.

"Pop the trunk. Let's get a look at this pooch," Cecil said.

When Gabe lifted the trunk, Luis couldn't help but feel uneasy. The girl he'd grabbed near L.A. Tradetech had now paled to the complexion of the whiteboy standing next to him.

"Hmmm. 'Bout five-one. Let's see. Maybe a hundred ten pounds. This one ought to be about an hour and thirty minutes. Pretty little squaw. What's it been about a couple hours? Something like that?" Cecil said.

"Yeah, Gabe said. "Something like that."

"Hell, I can strike up the furnace while both ya'll grab a quick turn," Cecil said. "She ain't gonna get all Catholic about anything now."

Gabe and Luis just stared at Cecil stoically.

"Ah, well. Just thought I'd throw it out there. She's going in the oven, anyhow," Cecil said. "Show me your money."

Gabe pulled out his wad, and pulled the last four bills off of the chrome clip.

"'Fraid that ain't gonna cut it, boys," Cecil said.

"Plus the three hundred we already gave you," Gabe said.

"Nah, nah, that there shovel is top o' the line," Cecil said. "Ya'll bought that for a fair price. No refunds."

Luis thought about pulling the starter pistol right then and there, and jamming it into the old man's rib cage.

"Minimum I take for a job like this is two thousand," Cecil said.

Gabe flashed Luis a look that said, we're gonna have to give him product.

Luis countered, with a look that said, no fucking way.

Cecil had a decisive grin. "What ch'all haulin'?"

Luis said, "Hey—"

"Crystal," Gabe said.

"Hot diggidy dawg," Cecil said. "What, ch'all got some biker crank?"

"Fuck, no," Gabe said. "Pure glass."

"Yo, I say we keep the body," Luis said. "Fuck this shit—"

Then, for some quizzical psychological reason, the Mexican boy, who was now livid, had lowered his voice, as though he couldn't see Cecil was right fuckin' there, and could here every fuckin' thing he said.

"We got to meet Lassiter in less than two hours," Luis hissed. "Yo, do not fuck with the product."

"We'll give you an eighth," Gabe said. "The shit's pure. After the girl's ashes."

"You'll give me an eighth now, boy." Cecil said. "And it better be whatchu say it is. Ain't no methamphetamine out there worth two grand for an eighth. Then, you'll give me another eighth, when the job's done."

"Deal," Gabe said.

Gabe handed Cecil a Ziploc of shards, and the old man slid the product into his pocket.

"Now let's get the body inside," Cecil said.

Luis looked at his watch, and back at Gabe.

"How long's it going to take to warm up the crematory?" Gabe said.

"Not long. 'Bout long enough for me to get real acquainted with your lady friend, here."

Gabe and Luis stripped Celina naked, then loaded her corpse onto the conveyor belt of a fairly modern crematory. There weren't any signs in front of Cecil's place indicating that it doubled as a funeral home. In fact, there weren't any signs at all. Gabe wondered why Cecil had invested in such a modern and likely expensive contraption.

"Folks come to me from fifty miles out. Sometimes a hundred. They bring me their pets. Cats, dogs. Even birds—although I don't charge nearly as much for birds. They all want their precious babies' ashes. Don't get too many instances like ya'll's," Cecil said. "Most people don't want a third party involved in cleaning up a murder."

Luis felt a chill, as they watched Cecil fire up the machine. Luisstared at Celina's thighs, her pussy and her tits. But not her face. He resisted the urge to cross himself.

The old man stopped the belt. Celina's body laid static, just short of the mouth of the incinerator. The machine roared. Gabe and Luis could feel the heat building.

"Well, it's about to get real hot in here, boys. Why don't ya'll wait for me in the main house. Just across the way," Cecil said. "I'll come getcha when she's done. Show you the ashes. There's a pool table in the house, if ya'll want to play with each other."

Gabe led the way, and Luis followed. As Luis went to close the door behind him, he saw the old man unfasten his belt buckle. He heard Cecil open his fly, and shuddered as he pulled the door shut, behind him. As soon as he heard it slam, Luis turned and vomited at the corner of the makeshift crematorium.

"Fuck, bro. You alright?"

"No. This is all some freaky shit. Look in the window," Luis said. "Tell me what you see."

Gabe walked up the three steps, and leaned to the right of the door. Inside he could see the old man's face, lit by a hellish glow from the crematory. His dirty jeans hung around his ankles, as his hips dug in with each thrust up against Celina's rubbery pale corpse. "Fuck." He pulled his head out of the window, before he could be seen.

"Let's just leave now," Luis said. "There's nothin' they can pin us on. No bullet or blood. Yo, she died of a heart attack, right? Now that fool's fuckin' her corpse. Let's just get the fuck out of here. This place scares the shit out of me."

"Yeah, maybe you're right," Gabe said.

The night was dark, but the moon was bright. Out in the desert you could see all the stars, too. Walking up to the main house, they could both see that the roof of the giant shack was covered with antennas, and a satellite dish. The shack was lit up like a Christmas tree, and likely wide open. There was still the matter of the lost eighth. They were still light, and country bumpkins never locked shit.

"Look at the size of that muthafuckin' dish, yo," Gabe said.

They exchanged a look, they both recognized as maybe the old man's got some shit we could steal.

The side door to the main house was open, and Gabe pulled on the knob.

Luis said, "They don't lock shit. Anyone could creep on these fools. Guess things are safer here in the country. What did cha'll do around here?"

"I wouldn't know, bro," Gabe said. "My old man left my moms when I was a kid, and she moved us to L.A. I ain't really from here, dawg. Only difference between you and me, is you got a scholarship, and my white ass gots to pay for the University of South Central with student muthafuckin' loans."

Inside the side door was a mud room. Several pairs of boots were lined up under a wall of garden tools. There were a stack of boxes next to the steps that lead into the shack. Luis read off the label on the side of one of the boxes. "What the fuck is Neeohdymeeum?"

"Let me see that shit," Gabe said, squatting down to read one of the labels. "Oh hell fuckin' yeah, bro. This is the shit they use—it's a metal—for smartphones. This shit is premium. This'll make up for lightening the load." The he lowered his voice—he wasn't sure why, but just out of paranoia. "I say we grab this shit, and then we're ghost from this freak fuck town."

The door to the main house swung open, and Gabe shot up to his feet. They both stared wide eyed at the doorway.

"Something I can help you boys with?"

The startling voice belonged to a stunner in daisy dukes, and combat boots, with a heather gray tee chopped off above the belly button. She had sweat patches between her tits, and below her pits, and they could feel the heat blowing from inside the house. "You boys cremating a pet?" she said.

"Yes, ma'am," Luis said, gesturing to Gabe. "His dog."

"Ya'll ain't got to call me ma'am. Hell, I ain't turned thirty yet. I'm Sierra," she said, glancing briefly at Gabe's crotch. "Why don't cha'll come inside. It's cold out here."

They could see she meant it. She had nipples like dimmer knobs.

The interior of the shack looked nothing like it did on the outside. They might've noticed a few peculiar items of décor— leather masks, and some odd looking medieval weapons, but instead they focused on the bottom of her ass cheeks poking out of those daisy dukes. Sierra walked them into a rumpus room that looked like it belonged in the Hollywood hills. There was a big rectangle-shaped bar that matched the lacquered hardwood floor, and a large, red felt pool table. Luis flashed Gabe a look that said, what the fuck are we going to do, now?

Sierra walked behind the bar. "Ya'll want a drink?"

Gabe shrugged. "Gin and juice."

"Tequila," Luis said.

"All we got is whiskey," Sierra said.

Sierra poured two shots, as Gabe looked glanced at one of several twisted looking paintings. To him it looked like that Vigo guy's painting, from *Ghostbusters II*. Disinterested, he looked away and took out his phone, as Luis eyes scanned the walls, taking in the peculiar artwork on the wall. He felt eyes on him.

There were a series of paintings, all of which had a vaguely ancient, religious look to them, but they were very different from any religious art he'd ever seen. Something about the angles, and the corners of the eyes and mouths. Something—

"Bottoms up," Sierra said, as Gabe turned to take the shot glass filled with brown liquid that was held out by three fingers on Sierra's right hand. When his eyes met her, he realized she was bottomless below the heather gray belly shirt, but still had her boots on. A black shrub with a Brillo pad's thickness couldn't hide the moisture from her enthusiasm. Gabe immediately pulled back in shock, as Luis turned toward the pool table, dropping his lower jaw, and beaming a sort of trance-like stare.

"You boys faggots? 'Cause I can't drink with no faggots," Sierra said, placing Luis's shot on the table near the corner pocket.

Gabe immediately downed his shot, and slammed it back down onto the edge of the pool table. Sierra grabbed his belt, worked it loose, and undid his fly. She grinned when she saw he was all ready to go. Gabe was helpless as she drew him in. When he was balls deep, he grabbed her thighs right under her cheeks, then spun her around, and put her back against the felt. She watched the innocent expression of shock morph into a look of pure aggression. Flared nostrils, a creased forehead and his thin lips drawn back to expose his teeth, as he grunted like a simian. The rumpus room echoed like a high school gym, and Luis heard every squelch, as Sierra laid her head down on the blood red felt. She turned her head toward Luis, and stared at him with a beaming gaze filled with lust. Her head rotated toward the ceiling, and her eyes clenched shut, as Gabe cried out *Oh God, oh God* over and over, as he exploded inside her.

Gabe pulled out, marveling at the oval wet stain on the red felt pool table. Sierra slid off of the pool table, soiled with Gabe's DNA. She picked up Luis's glass and sauntered over to him.

"Your shot," Sierra said, holding out the drink.

"I don't want it," Luis said.

"Are you a faggot?"

Luis said nothing.

She stepped closer. "Are you a faggot? I said, are you a fucking faggot?"

"Fucking puta!" Luis shouted, slapped the drink out of her hand, and they watched it smash onto the hardwood floor.

Sierra put her hand on his chest, and Luis froze. Then she worked it down slowly, to his belt, then his fly, and when she got her hands on him, he was harder than petrified wood. All she said was fuck me, over and over, until he pushed onto all fours and did her like the stray fucking perra she was. He took out the pistol, and slid it onto the floor, then gripped her hips like handlebars. Luis snarled and grunted obscenities, with every thrust, as Gabe stood a few feet away, voraciously stroking himself, while locking eyes with Sierra, under the ubiquitous gazes of oil painted demons.

By the time the earth shattering sound of the door opening from the outside shook the three of them, they were dressed, and had downed half a bottle of whiskey, at the bar.

Cecil walked in holding an urn the size of a mason jar. He leaned across the bar and gave Sierra a full open-mouthed kiss. "Hey, sweetie."

"Hey, Daddy," Sierra said sweetly.

Luis, far from sobered, held back the nausea.

"See you met my daughter," Cecil said, plunking the urn down onto the bar top. "There she is," he said with a light in his eyes, as if he were hiding a grin. "Now. There's the matter of full payment."

Three heavy sets of footfall, belonging to three solidly built men in their early thirties stopped short of the bar.

"These are my sons," Cecil said.

Each of the men held a small brick wrapped in plastic and duct tape. Luis felt the hair on the back of his neck stand up, as Gabe shot up off of his bar stool.

"Yo, what the fuck!" Gabe said.

"Ya'll really ought to keep your doors locked," Cecil said. His eyes kept a serious pitch, as one corner of his mouth curled up.

Luis's heart pounded, as his hands inched slowly around his back and into his waistband. He was so angry. So scared and so fucked, his eyelids were sweating.

"We made a fuckin' deal. One quarter," Gabe fumed. "That was the fucking deal!"

"How 'bout no quarter," Cecil said with a snicker. "You think you're the one that makes the rules, son. You little son of a whore."

"That shit you got ain't ours, old man," Gabe said. "And when the man come lookin' for us—whatever happens to us, I'm givin' him this place, and your fuckin' name."

Cecil laughed a sickly, maniacal laugh. Unfazed, he said, "Well now. We do love visitors."

His three sons joined in the old man's laughter.

Luis held the pistol still with his right hand, while he pulled on the rubber stopper at the end of the barrel with two fingers and the thumb on his left hand.

"Okay. Okay," Gabe said. "Just let us go. Keep the fuckin' product. Just let us go. We won't say shit. You got what you wanted."

Luis felt the rubber stopper pop off the end of the barrel.

"And you got what you wanted," Cecil said.

Gabe's palms were wet with sweat. His eyes darted over to Luis.

"Which one of ya'll fucked my daughter?"

Gabe had a guilty tell all over his face, as darkness fell over the twisted mugs of Cecil's menacing sons. Luis felt the sweat roll into his eyes as he wrapped his sweaty palm tightly around the handgrip of the pistol.

Sierra broke the silence. "They both did, Daddy. Fucked me good, too."

Luis bolted off the bar stool, and pulled the pistol, pointing it at the old man's forehead. "Don't fucking move."

The old man didn't flinch. "You ain't a killer, son."

"Now put the bricks on the bar top," Luis said. "Now!"

Still, nobody moved.

Luis pointed the starter pistol at the ceiling and fired. The shot echoed hellishly throughout the rumpus room. "Now!"

"Better do as he says," Cecil said.

Cecil's sons dropped the bricks one by one onto the bar top.

"Now get on your fucking knees," Luis said.

His three sons watched the old man chin a nod. Cecil's sons got on their knees.

"Grab the shit," Luis said, and Gabe scooped the bricks up in one armful. "Go!" Luis shouted and Gabe darted out of the rumpus room as Luis held the gun on the old man, who had yet to flinch. Luis backed away, his gun hand visibly shaking.

"Take me with you," Sierra gasped.

"Go!" Luis said, and Sierra was through the door. Luis started to back away.

"You look terrified, boy," Cecil said.

"You sick fuck freakshow motherfucker," Luis said.

"You have no idea." Cecil said. "How far you think you're going to get?"

Luis held the pistol firm, and with his free hand, he crossed himself.

"You puttin' a hex on me, boy?" Cecil said.

"He died for our sins. Evil motherfucker!" Luis said.

"Then that shall be his undoing," Cecil said calmly, and started to laugh, as Luis bolted for the front door.

The blast of cold air sobered him quick. Luis froze at the bottom of the shack's front porch, behind Gabe and Sierra. There in front of them sat Gabe's car, stripped down, propped up onto concrete blocks. Cecil's maniacal laughter followed them outside.

"You can toss that noisemaker away now, boy," Cecil said.

All three men heard the familiar charging sound of a pump

action shotgun. All three of them turned their heads in the direction of Cecil's voice. The man stood casually on the porch, a smile on his face, backlit by a hellish glow, as one of his sons held the barrel of the shotgun firm over the old man's left shoulder.

"Don't even think about runnin'. Cyrus here's a crack shot. And after that, well, you know where you're going," Cecil said. "Party ain't over, yet."

Cyrus held the shotgun firm. Luis tossed the starter pistol.

"Sierra," Cecil belted. "Come to Daddy."

Sierra slowly turned and walked over to the old man. He grabbed her firmly by the elbows and pulled her close. Then he grabbed her by the hair, pulled her head back, then pulled her in for a long passionate kiss, as his right hand dropped down and firmly palmed her ass cheek. She froze in defiance, and then reciprocated with wild abandonment. The old man pulled his mouth off hers, and stared into her eyes deeply.

"I'm so proud of you, sweetie," Cecil said. "You boys have done me a great service. For years I've been trying to get Sierra here pregnant. Tried my damn self, but the babies just didn't come out right. We just couldn't keep a child that weren't right. Believe it or not, finding a suitable donor ain't been exactly easy peasy. Sure there's been a few good lookin' stragglers come through town, willing to try and crème fill m'sweetie here. But there was always something—either they were firin' blanks, or they just weren't right. Even had a fellow last March on that ah, Feenest-ride. That stuff fellas take for hair loss. Made our boy pop off like he was pitching I-talian dressing, without the seasoning. But you boys. I watched ya'll crème fill my baby with blue cheese! Between the two of you, she go'n bring us a healthy grandbaby. I know what you're thinkin'. Got my boys here, but these boys, they're all homosexuals. I love my boys, but I just can't drink with 'em. Turn yourselves around, boys, and come inside. This party's just getting started."

* * *

"What'll it be?" the bartender said.

The man in black with the tattoo of a famous dog on his neck, looked down at the crack between her tits, and said. "Tequila."

"We only serve whiskey," the bartender said, lifting her chest with an encouraging grin.

"Best whiskey in Searchlight," the old man down the bar said. "You up here from L.A., son?"

"Yeah."

"What chu lookin' for out this way, son?"

"A girl," he said.

The old man perked up. "Maybe I can help you find her."

"I doubt it," the man in black said.

"You ain't a faggot are you, son?"

The man in black's dark eyes narrowed. The middle of his brow line dipped down, forging a menacing glare; hatred and vengeance all into one. The eyes of a killer. "Hell no, fool."

"That's what I like to hear," the old man said. "Can't drink with no faggots."

The bartender placed whiskey shots onto the bar top in front of the old man and the man in black. The old man held up his shot, and the man in black followed.

After they'd tossed 'em both back, the old man leaned over and said, "My name's Cecil. Yours?"

"They call me Little Snoopy."

PATRICIA ABBOTT is the author of *Concrete Angel*, *Shot in Detroit*, *I Bring Sorrow and Other Stories Of Transgression*, and *Monkey Justice*. She has been nominated for the Anthony, Edgar, and Macavity awards and won a Derringer for her flash story, "My Hero" She lives outside Detroit. You can find her at PattiNase.blogspot.com.

J.L. ABRAMO was born and raised in the seaside paradise of Brooklyn, New York, on Raymond Chandler's fifty-ninth birthday. Abramo is the author of *Catching Water in a Net*, winner of the St. Martin's Press/Private Eye Writers of America prize for Best First Private Eye Novel; the subsequent Jake Diamond Novels *Clutching at Straws*, *Counting to Infinity* and *Circling the Runway* (Shamus Award Winner); *Chasing Charlie Chan*, a prequel to the Jake Diamond series; and the stand-alone thrillers *Gravesend*, *Brooklyn Justice* and *Coney Island Avenue*. His latest novel is *American History*. Abramo is the current president of Private Eye Writers of America. For more please visit: JLAbramo.com.

JEN CONLEY'S short stories have been published in Beat to a Pulp, Thuglit, and many others. Her short story collection, *Cannibals: Stories from the Edge of the Pine Barrens*, was nominated for an Anthony Award in 2017. Her latest, *Seven Ways it Get Rid of Harry,* a YA novel about a thirteen-year-old boy who comes up with seven ways to get rid of his mom's cruel boyfriend, will be out in June 2019 from Down & Out Books. She lives in Brick, New Jersey. JenConley.net

JEFFERY HESS is the author of the novels *No Salvation*, *Beachhead*, and *Tushhog* and the short-story collection *Cold War Canoe Club* as well as the editor of the award-winning

Home of the Brave anthologies. He lives in Florida, where he leads the DD-214 Writers' Workshop for military veterans. Find or follow online at JefferyHess.com.

GRANT JERKINS is the award-winning author of five novels, including *A Very Simple Crime*, *At the End of the Road*, and *Abnormal Man*. His short story collection, *A Scholar of Pain*, is available now from ABC Group Documentation. He lives with his wife and son in the Atlanta area. GrantJerkins.com

DAVID JAMES KEATON'S fiction has appeared in over 100 publications, and his first short story collections: *Fish Bites Cop! Stories to Bash Authorities* and *Stealing Propeller Hats from the Dead*. His novels, *The Last Projector* and *Pig Iron* have also been optioned for film. Recently, he was the co-editor of the anthology *Hard Sentences: Crime Fiction Inspired by Alcatraz* and editor of *Dirty Boulevard: Crime Fiction Inspired by the Songs of Lou Reed*. He teaches composition and creative writing at Santa Clara University. DavidJamesKeaton.com.

ED KURTZ is the author of *The Rib From Which I Remake the World*, *Nausea*, *The Forty-Two*, and other novels. His short fiction has appeared in Thuglit, Needle, Shotgun Honey, and numerous anthologies including *Best American Mystery Stories* and *Best Gay Stories*. *Nothing You Can Do* is his first short story collection. Ed lives in Connecticut, where he is working on his next project.

R. DANIEL LESTER'S writing has appeared in multiple publications, including Shotgun Honey, Bareknuckles Pulp, The Flash Fiction Offensive, Switchblade, and Retreats from Oblivion: The Journal of NoirCon. His novella, *Dead Clown Blues*, was shortlisted for a 2018 Arthur Ellis Awards for Best Crime Novella by the Crime Writers of Canada. The follow up, *40 Nickels*, will be released in August 2019. Twitter: @rdaniellester

MARIETTA MILES'S short stories and flash can be found in Thrills, Kills and Chaos, Flash Fiction Offensive, Yellow Mama, Hardboiled Wonderland, Shotgun Honey and Revolt Daily as well as numerous anthologies. She is rotating host for Noir on the Radio, Dames in the Dark. She's had three book published: *Route 12, May,* and *After the Storm.* Born in Alabama, raised in Louisiana, she currently resides in Virginia with her husband and two children.

WARREN MOORE is Professor of English at Newberry College in Newberry, SC. His novel *Broken Glass Waltzes* was published by Down & Out Books in 2017, and his short stories have appeared in a variety of anthologies, webzines, and small press magazines. ProfMondo.wordpress.com

CHUCK REGAN writes genre fiction—military sci-fi, cosmic horror, retropunk action adventure, bizarro political satire, weird western, and everything in-between. His latest work-in-progress is a superhero noir series of novellas called *Stormkind.* To read samples from this and other projects, visit ChuckRegan.com.

SCOTCH RUTHERFORD writes about dark corners between the bright lights. An independent screenwriter and author, his work has appeared in Pulp Modern, The EconoClash Review, Pulp Metal Magazine, The Flash Fiction Offensive, Big Pulp, Shotgun Honey, and All Due Respect. He is the creator and managing editor of the outlaw digest magazine, *Switchblade.* He lives in L.A.

RYAN SAYLES is the Derringer-nominated author of the Richard Dean Buckner hard-boiled PI series, *The Subtle Art of Brutality, Warpath* and *Albatross* as well as the stand-alone novels *Goldfinches* and the forthcoming *Together They Were Crimson.* His short fiction has appeared in dozens of venues. He has been in numerous anthologies including the Anthony Award-nominated collections *Trouble in the Heartland: Crime Fiction Inspired by the Songs of Bruce Springsteen* and *Unloaded: Crime Writers Writing Without Guns.*

LIAM SWEENY is a writer and disaster responder from upstate New York. His work has appeared online and in print in such periodicals as Thuglit, Pulp Modern, Spinetingler Magazine, All Due Respect and The Flash Fiction Offensive. His collection of shorts, *Street Whispers* and the latest in his Jack LeClere detective series, *Presiding Over the Damned*, are loosed upon the world. LiamSweeny.com

RICHARD THOMAS is the award-winning author of seven books: *Disintegration, Breaker, Transubstantiate, Staring into the Abyss, Herniated Roots, Tribulations,* and *The Soul Standard.* Thomas has over 140 stories published. He received five Pushcart Prize nominations, was long-listed for Best Horror of the Year six times, and nominated for the Bram Stoker, Shirley Jackson, and Thriller awards. He's also edited four anthologies. In his spare time he is a columnist at Lit Reactor and Editor-in-Chief at Gamut Magazine. WhatDoesNotKillMe.com.

JAMES R. TUCK is the author of several novels, most notably the Deacon Chalk series, *Arrow: Fatal Legacies,* and *Venom: Lethal Protector.* He also writes the Mythos War series as Levi Black. He currently kicks ass in Denver, CO. JamesRTuck.com

LONO WAIWAIOLE is the only half-Hawaiian writer of noir crime fiction in the world. His six novels include *Dark Paradise,* an examination of the underside of his ancestral homeland and still the harshest light ever brought to bear on that topic. He writes full-time (now that he's too old to do much of anything else) in his adopted home of Portland, Oregon. He was previously a newspaper and magazine editor, a high school teacher and basketball coach, and a professional poker player. LonoWaiwaiole.com

On the following pages are a few
more great titles from the
Down & Out Books publishing family.

For a complete list of books and to
sign up for our newsletter,
go to DownAndOutBooks.com.

Deep White Cover
Joel W. Barrows

Down & Out Books
May 2019
978-1-948235-81-5

Extremist anti-immigrant groups and white-supremacist hate-mongers have begun to combine resources, and ideologies. These new hybrids of hate pose a rising threat, not only to the country's immigrants, but also to national security.

ATF Special Agent David Ward, undercover as a disgruntled veteran of the Army's Special Forces, works his way into *The Nation*, befriending its leaders and learning its secrets…or so he thinks. In truth, the organization's reach exceeds anything that the seasoned agent could have possibly imagined, something he will learn only when it seems too late to stop the revolution they seek.

Die Behind the Wheel
Crime Fiction Inspired by the Music of Steely Dan
Edited by Brian Thornton

Down & Out Books
June 2019
978-1-64396-016-6

What's the end result of a crazy scheme to match some of music history's most evocative and memorable songs with twelve of today's most entertaining writers? You're looking at it.

With this collection there's no need to chase the dragon, tour the Southland in a traveling minstrel show, or drink Scotch whiskey all night long. You've already bought the dream.

Covering every game in the Grammy-winning catalog of Donald Fagen and Walter Becker—collectively celebrated as Steely Dan—these compulsively readable stories will stagger the mind of ramblers, wild gamblers, and—of course—the winners in the world.

Countdown
Matt Phillips

All Due Respect, an imprint of
Down & Out Books
978-1-948235-84-6

LaDon and Jessie— two hustlers who make selling primo weed a regular gig—hire a private security detail to move and hold their money. Ex-soldiers Glanson and Echo target the cash—they start a ripoff business. It's the wild, wild west. Except this time, everybody's high.

With their guns and guts, Glanson and Echo don't expect much trouble from a mean son-of-a-gun like LaDon Charles. But that's exactly what they get. In this industry, no matter how much money there is for the taking—and no matter who gets it—there's always somebody counting backwards...to zero.

Main Bad Guy
A Love & Bullets Hookup
Nick Kolakowski

Shotgun Honey, an imprint of
Down & Out Books
978-1-948235-70-9

Bill and Fiona, the lovable anti-heroes of the "Love & Bullets" trilogy, find themselves in the toughest of tough spots: badly wounded, hunted by cops and goons, and desperately in need of a drink (or five).

After a round-the-world tour of spectacular criminality, they're back in New York. Locked in a panic room on the top floor of a skyscraper, surrounded by pretty much everyone in three zip codes who wants to kill them, they'll need to figure out how to stay upright and breathing...and maybe deal out a little pay-back in the process.

Made in the USA
Middletown, DE
08 January 2025

69021104R00146